Fighting from a Distance

THE ASIAN AMERICAN EXPERIENCE

Series Editors
Eiichiro Azuma
Jigna Desai
Martin F. Manalansan IV
Lisa Sun-Hee Park
David K. Yoo

Roger Daniels, Founding Series Editor

A list of books in the series appears at the end of this book.

Fighting from a Distance

How Filipino Exiles Helped Topple a Dictator

JOSE V. FUENTECILLA

UNIVERSITY OF ILLINOIS PRESS
Urbana, Chicago, and Springfield

Library of Congress Cataloging-in-Publication Data
Fuentecilla, Jose V.
Fighting from a distance : how Filipino exiles helped
topple a dictator / Jose V. Fuentecilla.
pages cm. — (The Asian American experience)
Includes bibliographical references and index.
ISBN 978-0-252-03758-0 (hardcover : alk. paper)
ISBN 978-0-252-07912-2 (pbk. : alk. paper)
1. Marcos, Ferdinand E. (Ferdinand Edralin), 1917–1989.
2. Movement for a Free Philippines (Organization).
3. Filipinos—United States—History.
4. Exiles—Political activity—United States.
5. Philippines—Politics and government—1973–1996.
6. Philippines—Foreign relations—United States.
7. United States—Foreign relations—Philippines.
DS686.5 .F84   2013
959.904'6   2013005910

Contents

Illustrations follow page 74

Preface

On May 19, 1973, a gathering of students and young professionals slowly filled the seats in the auditorium of the Holy Name School on West 97th Street in the New York City borough of Manhattan. Most were Filipinos and their American friends, drawn mainly by the news of events in Manila. Eight months earlier, on September 21, martial law had been declared by the president of the Philippines, Ferdinand Marcos.

Reports, both good and bad, traveled across the Pacific Ocean to confused relatives and friends in New York and other cities with large concentrations of Filipinos. There was peace and order in the homeland, they were told. In the meantime, because of the suspension of constitutional rule and the imposition of martial law, Marcos decrees were now the law of the land. The people filing into the auditorium felt the need to initiate some kind of collective response. As challenges to martial law spread in the Philippines, they moved to forge an overseas counterpart to the homegrown dissent. At that meeting, the outlines of an organized opposition took tentative form.

On September 22, almost a year to the day after the declaration of military rule, a national conference was convened, at which the first U.S.-based resistance to Philippine martial law was formally organized. It called itself the Movement for a Free Philippines—the MFP for short. The group named officers, issued resolutions, and formed committees. It placed an advertisement (5½ inches wide by 8½ inches deep) in the *New York Times* on September 27, announcing its formation (see illustrations). The ad appealed to the "Filipinos in the U.S. . . . to the American People . . . to the People of the Philippines," declaring the movement's intent to "work peacefully for the return of constitutional rule" to the Philippines. The MFP was soon followed by a number of other groups. Among the major ones were the Friends of the Filipino People (FFP) and the California-based Katipunan Ng Mga Demokratikong Pilipino (KDP)—the Union of Democratic Filipinos.

From the start, the leaders of these groups differed on goals and tactics. Strong personalities and deeply held political philosophies made consensus problematic. They were driven mainly by an abiding hatred for a dictatorship. They were focused on two goals: to expose the effects of martial law and to either cut or eliminate U.S. military aid to the Marcos regime. The members, mostly newly arrived immigrants who still had close ties to the Philippines, were acutely disturbed by the martial law directives that had muzzled the press, dissolved the legislature, jailed political opponents or driven them into exile, and outlawed organized dissent. They were witnessing a sudden shift to a state of affairs in their country that they had never experienced. These were new immigrants, most of whom had arrived during the late 1960s. They had spent the formative years of their lives under American tutelage after the liberation of their country from Japanese occupation in 1945. From the Americans they had learned the basic tenets of freedom and democracy. Now they were watching as their homeland's loss of those values was ignored by the same U.S. government that had made it possible for them to enjoy these freedoms. Also of concern were the uncertain fates of their families and friends back home under the new regime.

Who were those Filipinos who answered the call to gather in Manhattan on that spring day in 1973, and then a few months later came back together in larger numbers in Washington, D.C., to formally lay the foundations of a nationwide movement to resist the imposition of a new political order in their homeland? For the most part, they were two generations away from the first Filipinos who had come to the United States at the turn of the century. Their ancestors were the farmworkers who had toiled in the pineapple groves of Hawaii and the lettuce fields of California, the cannery workers at Alaska's fish factories, and the shrimpers on boats in Louisiana. By the 1960s and 1970s, this third generation included professionals who had entered through the urban immigrant gateways of the East and West Coasts. College students, medical workers, accountants, engineers, office workers—they swelled the Filipino population to close to a million. But beyond their numbers, they brought with them a life experience from the country that they had only recently left, but that had been virtually abandoned by the earlier Filipino settlers. True, many arrived as permanent economic migrants. Others intended their stay to be a temporary stopover while they accumulated skills and funds that they could eventually use back in the Philippines. Still others, a very small segment, found themselves exiled from home by virtue of being labeled enemies of the new regime in Manila.

Whether they considered themselves new immigrants or refugees or exiles, there was one overarching sentiment that impelled them to join the U.S.-based resistance movements: they were strongly troubled by the rise of a dictatorial regime in Manila, and they felt that they must organize to stop it. They could hear the rising voices of dissent there, and they understood that an overseas voice would be needed to amplify those messages. Fortuitously, they found themselves in a country from which they could safely launch their own resistance (although, as will be seen later, it was not an entirely safe refuge). By exposing the abuses of martial law to the American public, they intended to tap into the American belief in the primacy of human individual rights. The United States, they argued, had chosen to disregard these violations of human rights because the U.S. government placed a higher value on its vital economic and military interests in the Philippines. The next step would be to channel public displeasure toward their legislators, particularly the U.S. Congress. Hence lobbying for a reduction, if not elimination, of U.S. military aid to the Marcos regime was a major activity. They viewed this aid as the key prop that was keeping Marcos in power.

Even when their numbers were combined, the various opposition groups constituted only a fraction of the more than one million Filipinos in the United States during the 1970s. Early attempts to reach out to their compatriots were met with a general apathy toward participating in politically motivated activities. Fear of a backlash or retaliation from the Marcos regime was also a factor. To be sure, there was a vigorous Manila-based opposition to Marcos that inspired their U.S.-based counterparts. Over the fourteen years of martial law, resistance activity flourished. Students, farmers, religious groups, politicians, professionals, and working-class populations came out against the Marcos regime. Most prominent were Marxist-inspired insurgents, fired by an ideology and emboldened by an armed guerrilla cadre. But they were all vulnerable to swift retribution from the regime. In contrast, the U.S.-based opposition groups knew that being an ocean away provided them some degree of safety. Despite the distance, as taxpaying and voting citizens, they were well placed to influence events in the Philippines.

A large part of this history is taken up by the experience of the MFP. The movement was led by Raul S. Manglapus, a former Philippine senator and foreign secretary. Having had a long career in government service, he had a sterling reputation that earned him a large following among Filipinos during his fourteen-year involuntary stay in the United States. An eloquent speaker, scholar, and lawyer, he reached out to a wide circle of American foreign policy makers. His tireless lobbying, prolific writings in U.S. publications, and speeches to various groups further enhanced the MFP's visibility. As a result, the MFP emerged as the primary mover in the opposition movement. Unlike some of the other groups, the MFP was no monolithic fraternity bonded by a single political ideology. On the contrary, the disparate personalities of its leaders were bound together by one overarching commitment—the overthrow of a Philippine dictator. The question of how to accomplish that goal resulted in intermittent squabbles.

During the last half of the twentieth century, immigrant groups in the United States played both major and minor roles in overthrowing authoritarian governments in their homelands. The role of political exiles in achieving regime changes has been well documented. Exiles contributed to the downfall of the Nazis in Germany and the fascists in Italy during World War II. Charles de Gaulle's exile organization in London, Free France, helped liberate occupied France from the Nazis. Between 1970 and 1990, exiles were also part of the struggle for democratic change in Chile, Argentina, Brazil, and South Korea. The Arab Spring protesters of 2011, partly encouraged by their internet-connected diaspora compatriots and sympathizers around the world, are only the latest incarnation of this movement.

Ethnic exiles in the United States have been engaged in ongoing efforts to isolate their home-based adversaries in Cuba, Northern Ireland, and Palestine. Brett Heindl's study of political activists in American, Cuban, Jewish, and Irish communities in the U.S. demonstrates how these "ethnic activists bring a single-mindedness and intensity to foreign affairs with few equivalents. Whether their actions take the form of lobbying, remittance-sending, or acts of violence, exile and diaspora groups' efforts to make political change in their ancestral homelands have far-reaching implications for the success or failure of . . . homeland reform and opposition movements."[1] For example, Heindl cites Irish immigrants in the second half of the nineteenth century who raised money to ship arms to support various independence movements. Immigrants from Israel, Mexico, Haiti, the Dominican Republic, Croatia, and Poland used their ability to vote in homeland elections to exert direct electoral influence over homeland politics. During the Cold War, expatriate Cubans and Nicaraguan "contras" were trained on U.S. soil to counteract Castro's Communist regime and the Nicaraguan Sandinista government.

Fighting Marcos from a distant shore would prove to be a learning experience for the U.S.-based Filipino groups. How they persevered provides a lesson in organizing and sustaining efforts to overthrow a well-entrenched enemy. They took a page from Gene Sharp's remarkable handbook *From Dictatorship to Democracy*, a guide to the nonviolent overthrow of repressive regimes. Sharp cautions that "the main force of the struggle must be borne from inside the country itself. To the degree that international assistance comes at all, it will be stimulated by the internal struggle."[2] The internal struggle by homegrown oppositionists has been well documented. It is the external assistance, such as the role of the Filipino political activists in the United States—small in numbers and splintered in their solidarity—that has not been fully told. This book is their story.

CHAPTER 1

The First Exiles

Escaping from the Homeland

On September 22, 1972, a nationwide dragnet swept up hundreds of Filipinos deemed hostile to the sudden imposition of martial law that day. They included politicians, journalists, civil rights activists, lawyers, and suspected members of the Communist-leaning insurgent New People's Army. In the days to come, more people would be apprehended and moved to detention centers. President Marcos declared that this drastic action was necessary because these sectors had all threatened to overthrow the government. Months earlier, escalating street protests, riots, and strikes had been characterized as a plot to destabilize the government. As early as August 24, Marcos had vowed in a nationwide address to impose martial law in order to "liquidate [the] Communist apparatus." On September 8, Defense Secretary Juan Ponce Enrile warned that Communists were threatening terrorist attacks in Manila "24 hours a day."

Marcos had been impelled to act, it was reported, because of an assassination attempt on Enrile while he was reportedly riding in his car in the late evening of September 22. Senator Raul Manglapus was in a Tokyo hotel on September 23, on his way to California for a series of speaking engagements, when he read about the assassination attempt in the *Japan Times*. He had left Manila the previous afternoon. What follows is a slightly edited account of that day, which Manglapus wrote on October 15, 1983, in Washington, D.C. This account appears in *A Pen for Democracy*, a compilation of published articles, letters, and U.S. congressional testimonies compiled by the Movement for a Free Philippines. It omits details about how those who managed to escape the dragnet made it out of the country, because when it was written, Marcos was still in full control, rounding up more suspects. (By November 16, more than six thousand had been arrested.)[1] Manglapus did not want to divulge the escape routes through unnamed places and countries. For the same reason, some of those who assisted him in evading arrest remain unidentified.

The phone rang in [my] hotel room [in Tokyo].

It was my wife [Pacita LaO or Pacing]. She had luckily managed to reach me before the overseas lines were cut. "Vamos a hablar en espanol," she said quickly. It was the only code she could think of in a country where the Hispanic tongue has all but disappeared except in our Christian and last names. She told me that what I thought would not yet happen, had happened; that martial law had been declared the night before and that soldiers had come to our house to arrest me at 1:30 in the morning. Also, that the soldiers, being told I was away, had not believed it and that they had searched the house for two long hours, opening every door, "including the door to the refrigerator."

She said that soon after the soldiers left, she received a call from Judy Roxas, wife (now widow) of Senator Gerry Roxas, who asked if I could join in forming a legal panel for the release of Senator Benigno Aquino, Senator Jose Diokno, and others who had all been arrested at precisely 1:30 that morning.

"I am sorry, Raul is not here," my wife had replied, "and besides, the soldiers also came to pick him up at 1:30 this morning."

My first impulse was to return home immediately, but my wife would not hear of it. "Why should you come home straight to jail? Go on to the United States. Maybe you can do something there about this."

I protested, "What about you? When will I see you and the children again? And besides, I have money for only ten days!"

"You'll find a job," she insisted, "and don't worry about us. We can take care of ourselves."

When she finally hung up, I could not hold back the tears. I was facing the bleak prospect of a long separation from my family. I was neither emotionally nor financially ready for an extended exile. And there was another immediate problem—although I was supposed to be an expert in foreign relations, I had no idea how far Marcos would or could go in getting me back to the Philippines. Could

Marcos, for instance, persuade the Japanese government to bundle me into a Philippine Air Lines plane to Manila? Or, if I managed to leave Tokyo for the United States, would the U.S. government turn me back at Honolulu?

My son [Toby, who had graduated from Tokyo's Sophia University] came up from Fukuoka, in Southern Japan, where he was training at the Matsushita Training Center. We discussed the situation and decided to seek help. I called Shigeharu Matsumoto, the distinguished director of the International House of Japan, who had more than once invited me to Tokyo for speaking engagements. Then I telephoned an American friend, a former classmate at Georgetown Law School in Washington, D.C., who was living in Honolulu with his wife, a Filipino doctor. He agreed to help me through United States immigration and customs.

Mr. Matsumoto came to my hotel with his entire family. They took my son and me to the airport and made sure I got to the right plane to Honolulu. I bade a sad goodbye to my son and took off. Either Marcos was too busy to get me back, I thought to myself, or it simply is not legally possible to do so. I was just beginning to learn by experience the stricter applications of international law on political refugees.

In Honolulu, my American classmate who had been a United States federal officer managed to get me port courtesies. I stayed with my friend and his wife for a week, stunned, groping my way through the first stages of life in exile. The first two days I spent almost entirely in bed, staring at the ceiling, unable to make decisions. On the third day, I decided to call William P. Bundy, former U.S. assistant secretary of state for East Asia and the Pacific, whom I had met while I was a senator. I asked him to help me get a job. He called Dr. Harlan Cleveland, then president of the University of Hawaii. Dr. Cleveland invited me to breakfast and promised to look for a position for me at the University. However, I later decided that if I was to live an effective life of exile, I should be near the two centers of American power—New York City and Washington, D.C., just as a century ago the Filipino propagandists of our revolution against Spain had chosen to be around Madrid and Barcelona.

Finally in San Francisco, I met Sister Reina Paz, a Maryknoll sister from the province of Occidental Negros, who had invited me in May of 1972 to come to speak at the inauguration of the Philippine

Center in Stockton, California, in August. I told her gratefully had it not been for you, I would be in prison. She worried about me. She was plagued with a mixed feeling: of relief that her invitation had occasioned my evading arrest, and guilt that it had thrust me, quite unprepared, into confrontation with an uncertain life of exile.

I then proceeded to New York City, where I made new friends among those in the Filipino-American community who were willing to deal with a "hunted" man. I subleased an efficiency apartment from a Filipino couple and learned to steam rice and cook such basic Filipino dishes as "nilaga" and "sinigang."

When martial law was declared, General Carlos P. Romulo was in New York City heading the Philippine delegation to the United Nations General Assembly. Learning I was in New York, he sent his daughter-in-law, Mariles Cacho Romulo, to look for me and to invite me to see him.

I had been close to the Romulos since I first served under then Major Romulo as broadcaster in the press relations office of General [Douglas] MacArthur's USAFFE headquarters at the outbreak of the Pacific War [World War II]. When General Romulo landed back in Leyte [province] with General MacArthur on October 20, 1944, I was with the Romulo family in Pagsanjan, in the province of Laguna, where I had evacuated my mother after my escape from Japanese prison two months before. Mrs. Virginia Romulo opened her last can of imported fruit salad to celebrate her husband's landing as well as my birthday, which coincidentally was on that same day.

After the liberation of Manila [from the Japanese], General Romulo had me appointed chief of the Radio Division of the office of President Sergio Osmena Sr. Later, in 1947, I would come to Washington, D.C., to study law at Georgetown University and attempt to conclude my courtship of my childhood friend Pacita LaO, who, with her mother, was also in Washington, D.C., visiting her sister and her brother-in-law, Col. Jaime C. Velasquez, then military attaché at the Philippine Embassy.

When Pacing and I decided to get married in Washington, it was General Romulo who called the Apostolic Delegate, Amleto Cardinal Cicognani, to ask him to officiate at our small wedding at the elegant chapel to the Apostolic Delegation (where Pope John Paul II would stay for his historic 1982 visit) on Massachusetts Avenue. Bobby, the youngest of the four Romulo sons, was our ring bearer. When Carlos Romulo Jr., who was later to die in a plane crash, had his first son by his bride Mariles, I was asked to be the baptismal sponsor.

Thus it was with the confidence of a fellow Democrat and a close family friend that I took the elevator up with my comadre Mariles to General Romulo's Waldorf-Astoria suite in Manhattan. After he told me how much he regretted Marcos's repression of the people and the suppression of the Philippine press which he loved so much, I told him that I felt he would make an ideal leader for an exile movement in the United States, since at least one generation of Americans still remembered him as the Voice of Freedom.

He was going home to Manila, he said, only to "put his things together" and then come back to the United States. I understood this to mean he would come back to lead the exiles' struggle for the return of democracy.

General Romulo came back indeed—not to lead the exiles, but as a defender of the Marcos dictatorship. Marcos had succeeded in enlisting him in lending credibility to the new tyranny before the American people.

It became necessary to look for another leader, and soon it was evident that by default the mantle would fall on me. I was ready to lead even if my wife and family were still back home. But first I was going to try to get them out of the country.

I learned that Pacing had gone to Juan Ponce Enrile, Marcos's defense minister, and had been refused permission to leave. From Cornell University in upstate New York, where Bill Bundy had secured for me a fellowship with a grant from the Ford Foundation, I came down to Washington to talk to several senators about appealing to Marcos to allow my family to join me here as a humanitarian gesture. Among those who agreed to help me were Senators Hubert Humphrey, Ted Kennedy, and Charles Percy. All were turned down by Marcos.

Senator Humphrey's office furnished me with a copy of Enrile's reply on behalf of Marcos. It was an amusing piece. While [Marcos's wife] Imelda's "Blue Ladies," her coterie of sycophants, were traipsing around the world consuming foreign exchange, my wife and family, said Enrile, could not be permitted to leave because "considering [my] stature in the community, the whole matter will in no time become public knowledge as an exception case and would therefore tend to destroy our image of sincerity and impartiality which we are steadfastly aiming to preserve."

It was evident that Marcos's coup plans had not counted on the formation of a free exile movement, and they were now going to keep my family as hostages to keep me gagged abroad. So it was suggested to Senator Humphrey that "ex-Senator Manglapus be persuaded to return to the Philippines," concluding that "if after having returned he would still think as he now plans, of transferring himself and his entire family to the United States, the matter would be given most sympathetic consideration and understanding at that time."

"Senator," Dan Spiegel, Senator Humphrey's legislative aide, told me with a meaningful smile as he handed me the copy of Enrile's reply, "I hope you won't fall for that last part."

"Don't worry," I replied, "I won't."

I had remained in touch with my wife by telephone. She would move from house to house in Manila to elude phone tapping. After returning to Cornell from Washington, I told her that I had exhausted all overt means of getting her and the family over. She would have to try something else.

Yes, she replied that "something else" was already in the works. She was planning her escape.

It was Maria Teresa "Boots" Anson (now Mrs. Jerry Jumat) organizer of the Christian Social Movement (CSM) for northern Luzon, who first approached my wife with a definitive plan of escape.[2]

The escape plan called for quick and dangerous execution, and on March 21, 1973, Pacing and my three sons, Raul Jr. (Raulito), Roberto (Bobby), and Francis Xavier, aided by a combined Christian-Muslim group, found themselves island-hopping to a third country. My only daughter, Tina, just married to Ben Maynigo, elected to stay behind. For continuing security reasons, not too much detail can now be revealed about the escape.

I can say a little of the harrowing early morning of March 26, 1973, when the telephone rang in my apartment (No. 3F, Fairview Heights, Cornell University) at 3:00 A.M.

"Is this Mr. Manglapus?" a girl's voice.

"Yes."

"Go ahead, please . . ."

"Hello . . ."

"Yes?"

"Mr. Manglapus?" a man with a slight Chinese accent.

"Yes, yes . . ."

"This is Father (fade . . .)"

"Who?"

"Father_____in_____ "

"Oh?"

"Your son Bobby . . ."

"Yes, yes, I have a son named Bobby . . ."

"Your son Bobby asked me to call you."

"Yes?"

"Your wife and sons are in a boat at the docks. The authorities refuse to let them land."

"Oh no! What's the problem?"

"They came thinking there was no need for a landing pass. But this is required. Can you help them?"

"Yes, yes. I will do what I can."

"They are being given only a few days."

"Is there any danger they might be sent back?"

"I don't know."

"Oh my God! Give me your phone number, please—and beg the authorities not to send them back! I'll start making calls . . ."

Start making calls? At three o'clock in the morning? What decent American, the kind that can best be of help, would be awake? Even mad dogs and Englishmen are asleep at this hour!

Ah, but halfway around the world, it is three in the afternoon! Think. Who do I know in that third country? Don't panic. Think. Yes, yes—the president of the university. I visited him once. And his wife came to visit us in Makati [a suburb of Manila]. Call him. He'll help.

"Sorry, he's out of town."

"How about Mrs. _____?"

"She's also out of town."

Don't remember anybody else important in that country. What about the neighboring "fourth" country? Maybe they have a consul in the area who can extend protection.

I called friends there, mostly journalists, and they all promised to help. I was to learn some years later their foreign minister had alerted his consuls around the area to extend a humanitarian hand to my family, transcending political considerations. But as my journalistic friends had insisted, it was not their territory, and it would have had to take direct intervention by the government of the third country to save my family.

Finally, at nine o'clock that morning I reached Bill Bundy on the phone. He promptly went to work, calling the U.S. State Department and his friends in the third country. After some hesitation, the third country government agreed to move my family to their capital, where they were kept in a comfortable home away from public view. After still more hesitation, the State Department agreed to process them for entry into the United States. The political issue was skirted by considering them not as political refugees but as dependents of an alien with a working visa, which I had obtained upon moving to Cornell.

Pacing and the boys landed at Kennedy Airport in New York City on April 6, 1973. They had blazed an escape trail which others would follow later: in 1976 my daughter Tina, her husband Ben Maynigo, her own baby daughter Tanya, and her husband's cousin and housekeeper Perpedigna Bugyong, together with the couple who were the principal planners and executors of the original escape—Jerry and Boots Jumat, accompanied by their children Lara and Wally; in 1978 Bonifacio Gillego, retired Philippine army intelligence officer who was deputy secretary-general of the CSM and my fellow delegate and trusted associate in the Constitutional Convention, followed by Charito Planas, noted woman lawyer who had been a mayoralty candidate in Quezon City [a suburb of Manila]; and in 1980 Gaston Ortigas, dean of the Harvard-sponsored Asian Institute of Management in Manila and chairman of the CSM Manila chapter, followed by his cousin, Fluellen Ortigas, a brilliant youth leader who had been in and out of political prison.

Barely a month after my family's arrival, the Movement for a Free Philippines (MFP) was organized in a public meeting at the Holy Name School auditorium in Manhattan, New York. In September 1973, it was formalized at a convention in Washington, D.C. I was elected president.

In 1980, when Senator Benigno Aquino was allowed to come to the United States for a heart bypass operation, I offered to step aside so that the MFP might elect him president. He declined.[3]

CHAPTER 2

Rough Landings

Surviving the First Years

Manglapus's family's escape took seventeen days, a measure of the ordeal that would-be escapees faced. Martial law security forces were extra-vigilant regarding people with the stature and the means to pose problems for the Marcos regime. Hence, even family members and close associates of prominent activists felt that they were under surveillance, especially those who had evaded arrest by "going underground" locally or who had somehow made it out of the country.

Escape routes out of the Philippine archipelago were either by air or by sea. Some people took what became known as "the back door"—island-hopping from Zamboanga province on the southern tip of Mindanao Island to Malaysia. Manglapus's family—his wife disguised in a wig, and carrying false identification papers—managed to slip out of their home in Urdaneta village in Manila and make it to the airport. From Zamboanga, a motorboat took them to Sibutu Island, off Sabah, a Malaysian state. There, the authorities refused to allow them to disembark because they had no landing permit. While Manglapus contacted friends for help, they sat bobbing on the water for three days. "It was a *kumpit*, a motorized boat with bamboo outriggers. At least it had a roof. But no bathroom," Pacita remembered. "One more day on this boat and I'll go back home," Raulito joked in frustration.[1] It had taken them days to get to this point; they were almost ashore, and now they found themselves stranded. Once they were finally on land, they proceeded to Kota Kinabalu, the capital of Sabah; then to Kuala Lumpur, the main capital; and then onward to Singapore, Istanbul, Cairo, Athens, and New York. Ben Maynigo's family followed essentially the same sea route, but their journey took a frightening turn when their boat was chased by pirates. An armed escort arranged by the Jumats, who were on the same boat, got them safely to Malaysia.

The anxious months spent hatching schemes to escape, compounded by the perils of the trip, were bad enough. Getting settled as an exile proved to be the real struggle. Manglapus, like other prominent Marcos opponents, had a wide circle of friends who provided temporary support. But for those without such a safety net, economic survival was of paramount concern. Charito Planas, a lawyer and former candidate for mayor of Manila, was a well-connected leader of various civic organizations and political groups in the Philippines, living a comfortable cosmopolitan life. She arrived in Virginia on June 5, 1978. At one time, home was a basement, furnished with wares salvaged from flea markets and the streets. Unable to obtain gainful employment, she worked as a telemarketer; ran a pizza parlor, even delivering the pizzas herself; demonstrated food preparation at shopping malls; and delivered parcels.[2] Bonifacio Gillego, former deputy secretary-general of the CSM and a delegate to the Constitutional Convention of 1971–72, worked as a security guard and as a hotel accountant in Washington, D.C. Friends who visited Gaston Ortigas in 1981 "found not the well-heeled professor of management they knew in Manila but a gaunt man living on coffee and cigarettes in a little home office on Rivera St. off Sunset Boulevard in San Francisco."[3]

Heherson Alvarez, a lawyer who was elected a delegate to the Constitutional Convention, went into hiding soon after martial law was declared. Former president Diosdado Macapagal, whom he had served as private secretary, advised him to flee overseas and join Manglapus. He made it to Hong Kong, where the captain of a cargo ship sneaked him aboard in November 1972 as a stevedore. He was directed by friends to a small printing shop, where he had been told that for 5,000 Hong Kong dollars he could obtain a fake passport (a week later, the pickup price had increased to 50,000 HK dollars). After a few test trips to Macau to acquire authentic entry stamps on its pages, it got him into France, Canada, and then the United States, and into temporary housing with Manglapus.

The first exile who succumbed to the stressful anxieties of being stranded was another high-ranking government official. Raoul Beloso, the chairman of the Small Farmers Commission of the Department of Agriculture, was attending a conference in New York when martial law was declared. He fired off an angry letter to President Richard Nixon that was printed in the *New York Times,* in which he warned of the advent of a "police state" and an "absolutist regime." He then founded a group called Filipinos for Freedom, which was affiliated with the MFP. He proposed "an action group to help in the legal defense of deserving Filipinos who have applied for political asylum," presenting his successful asylum case as "a precedent for others to invoke."[4] Eventually, however, feeling homesick, missing his wife, and broke (he tried unsuccessfully to sell insurance), he yearned desperately to return to the Philippines. But he had crossed a bridge. If he should return, he feared that Manila would trumpet his "defection." It would be seen as a defeat for his "freedom" group. He could not bear the thought of promising the regime that he would publicly retract his letter in the *New York Times* in exchange for safe passage. On April 6, 1975, he hanged himself in his small apartment on Broadway in Manhattan. He was forty-nine years old.

The Philippine consulate in New York ordered the medical examiner not to release Beloso's suicide note, ruling his death a result of "foul play." The lawyer representing his next of kin had to go to the New York Supreme Court to obtain a copy. In it, Beloso affirmed that he would not "surrender to the Dictator." Loida Nicolas Lewis, a Filipino lawyer based in New York, said that the "government has reason to obfuscate the suicide of Mr. Beloso and to suppress his final letter. His act and his letter are Raoul Beloso's final political statement of protest."[5]

In 1975, Manglapus's own financial situation turned gloomy. A year earlier, he had obtained a position as a visiting professor and senior research associate at Cornell University in New York. That job was now coming to an end, and he "was not sure where [he would] find a new one . . . Trickles [of funds] from Manila had stopped." All three boys were in college; Bobby and Francis were at Cornell, where the costs for both exceeded $15,000 a year, whereas Manglapus's take-home pay from Carnegie was barely more than $20,000. To make ends meet, Pacing ran a children's daycare center in their residence. In a letter to Bobby and Francis, he warned them that they might have to drop out of school and look for jobs. Raulito was facing the same prospect. "If we pull together," Manglapus wrote, "we will manage to see this through and get you your education. But you will have to help. I am sorry that I cannot do better. Perhaps one day something will turn up that will make things look brighter. But it is not yet in sight."[6]

The Carnegie Endowment for International Peace, based in Manhattan, eventually offered Manglapus a position as a senior associate in its International Fact-Finding Center program. The director, Charles Maynes, said that the post was designed to provide "outstanding foreign affairs specialists an opportunity to study pending international conflict situations and produce policy-relevant reports."[7] While at Carnegie, Manglapus applied for a fellowship with the Woodrow Wilson International Center for Scholars in Washington, D.C.

Maynes approved his study proposal on non-Western democratic traditions. Because the International Fact-Finding Center is partly financed through congressional appropriations, the U.S. State Department exercised its leverage as a member of the board. The department's Office of Philippine Affairs stated that "it was deemed inappropriate for the U.S. Government to appear to be subsidizing a person who is actively engaged in activities directed against a government with which the U.S. Government enjoys friendly relations."[8] The board vetoed Manglapus's application. In a letter to U.S. Ambassador to the Philippines William Sullivan, Maynes objected that the rejection was "dictated by political concerns, not academic merit," adding that not only was it "incredibly petty for the State Department to prevent a former Foreign Secretary who has been friendly to the United States to pursue scholarly activities," but it was also "politically unwise since at some point this kind of official pressure is bound to come to the attention of the Congress with acute embarrassment for all concerned."[9] Manglapus applied again the next year, and for some reason the department had "progressed to a passive position," wrote *Chicago Sun-Times* columnist Charles Bartlett. "The official line goes 'We don't think it's a good idea but we won't fight it if the fellowship is voted by the board.'"[10] By that time, Manglapus's proposal had been accepted by the New York–based human rights advocacy group Freedom House, for which he received a grant.

There had been an earlier episode in 1973 to block a fellowship grant, that time from the Ford Foundation. Marcos must have learned about it, because "he tried to pull the grant from under me by availing of [chairman Henry Ford's wife] Cristina Ford's friendship with Imelda," said Manglapus.[11] In a biography of Ford by Victor Lasky, the author wrote that Henry Ford himself had contacted the directors of the Ford Foundation about the grant. "Asked about this by the *Washington Post*, the Ford Motor Company confirmed that in 1973 the Chairman 'did receive an inquiry on Mr. Manglapus.'"[12] The foundation "rejected Henry Ford's soundings for a review," Manglapus said. But he found it "curious," Lasky wrote, "that his fellowship, amounting to $12,000 out of total disbursements that year exceeding $100 million, had been personally reviewed" by Ford.[13] In his column, Bartlett wrote that "Manglapus did not find a particularly warm reception in this country because people and institutions preferred to keep their relations with Manila." It was a mindset that Manglapus deplored:

> In politics, the old saw goes, there are no friends—only allies. But in exile we exiles, we are not really in politics but in the universal struggle for democracy and human rights. Among our friends and allies are members of the United States Senate and House of Representatives, their aides, sympathetic U.S. government officials, American churches, organizations and individuals. The most potent bloc of sympathizers is perhaps the U.S. media.
>
> Our only real enemy in America is a state of mind—that myopic, condescending, indeed criminal notion that democracy and human rights are a Western invention which is sometimes unsuited to non-Western cultures and must be sacrificed for the sake of the brittle "stability" of dictatorships necessary for the military and economic interests of the United States of America. Many U.S. policy makers are still locked into this state of mind.[14]

It must be noted that by holding the Manglapus family hostage, Marcos was able to muzzle an opponent who he knew would likely lead an exile opposition group. Indeed, during the almost six months that they were held, Manglapus had to hold his fire lest they be harmed. A number of his more vigorous anti-Marcos Senate colleagues were among the first to be imprisoned. As soon as his family was out of the president's clutches, he fired his first salvo—a speech titled "Facts and Fiction about Martial Law" at the University of Michigan in Ann Arbor on April 17, 1973. Over the next thirteen years, across the country and in Europe, his would be the most prominent voice denouncing the Marcos regime.

CHAPTER 3

Into the Land of the Fearful

Dread and Apathy

Much of the print coverage of the U.S.-based anti-Marcos groups tended to spotlight prominent exile figures. Having found the freedom to speak out, to write for publication, to demonstrate, to organize openly—activities that could get their colleagues back home in trouble with the authorities—they plunged into furious rounds of organizing the resident Filipino population. They arrived as eyewitnesses, with personal experience of what martial law was like on the ground. It was not derived from the U.S. news correspondents or from the Philippine-controlled media or from secondhand accounts. They had assumed that their compatriots in the United States would empathize with their experience and respond readily to appeals for money, membership, and participation. They were shocked to discover that such was not always the case.

Anti–martial law activists who reached out to Filipino communities were met with two reactions—apathy and fear. Apathy was most pronounced among the newer immigrants. They had come to the United States to improve their prospects for a livelihood they found unachievable back in the Philippines. The first order of business was to get settled—employment, housing, education for their children—all the basics of survival in their new home. There was no room to indulge in politics, local or Philippine. Concepts of human rights, "U.S. imperialism," and congressional authorizations of foreign aid were as distant from their minds as the wide oceans that separated their countries.

There was also the fear of getting involved. News of roundups, interrogations, and military detentions was constant. They would not want to jeopardize relatives back home once their U.S. activities were made known. A California-based Filipino weekly, the *Philippine News*, published the names of some 150 Filipino residents of the United States whom the Philippine government had accused of being anti–martial law activists.[1] Consulates were instructed not to renew their passports. The details revealed about their affiliations with groups and organizations showed just how closely the Filipino community was being watched by the authorities back home. Indeed, the scope of the list was stunning. It showed that the government would not spare even those with the flimsiest of ties to "activities abroad which are detrimental to the national interests." A number of people were identified simply as "reported activists." The coded list was obtained by Consul General Ruperto Baliao of the Philippine consulate in Los Angeles. Disgusted, he resigned his post on May 18 "to protest the dictatorial policies of Marcos," becoming the first of several high-profile defectors. The "blacklist," as it came to be known, had been transmitted by Manila to the Philippine ambassador in Washington, D.C., on April 25 and April 26, 1973.[2]

Also blacklisted was Alex Esclamado, the editor of the *Philippine News*, which at that time was the most widely circulated Filipino newspaper in the United States critical of the martial law regime. He wrote that the list was "composed mostly of writers and editors of Filipino-American newspapers and magazines, radio announcers, student leaders and heads of community organizations." The decoded messages to Baliao instructed him to cancel Esclamado's passport and those of "all members of his staff. Make representation with local authorities, if necessary, to get their cooperation to ensure implementation of this order and take such other steps as will compel their return to the Philippines."[3] Targeting Esclamado and the *Philippine News* was a calculated move, intended to scare the larger Filipino community. The newspaper had been one of the most outspoken critics of Marcos's policies even before martial law. Its California advertisers were now being pressured by Manila to withdraw their financial support.

Baliao's defection had caused considerable furor in Filipino communities. The *Philippine News* reported that "he was regarded by . . . many circles here as a loyal and devoted Philippine government official."[4] As the highest-level official Philippine representative in the city where the greatest number of Filipinos resided, his turnaround was big news as much as the blacklist. In a coordinated move to prevent any more such incidents, the Philippine government announced that it was renegotiating a package of military and trade treaties with the United States. According to Baliao, the package included a possible extradition pact—"a sword of Damocles over the heads of Filipinos in the U.S."[5] Implicit was the threat of extradition for Marcos enemies.

In his first public address in New York City, on May 19, 1973, at the Holy Name School, Manglapus sought to dampen the fear that had spread as a result of the blacklist and the extradition threat. "Cancellation of passports, revocation of visas, even extradition are . . . childish threats . . . ignore them because they are idle."[6] He reminded his audience that the United States was a signatory to a United Nations convention that protected political refugees, prohibiting the expulsion or return of refugees to their country if their lives or freedom would be threatened there because of their race, religion, nationality, or membership in a particular group or political party. But the fear persevered and posed organizing and recruitment problems.

There was always the lingering suspicion that the opposition groups were being infiltrated by Philippine government agents. Gillego, a retired army major and military intelligence officer with the Armed Forces of the Philippines and an MFP officer, cited suspicious incidents directed against MFP officers—the garbage cans at the San Francisco residence of Steve Psinakis had been ransacked; threats had been made against Dr. Jojo Villalon in Chicago and Dr. Arturo Taca in St. Louis; the home of Willie Crucillo in New York had been burglarized; and MFP documents had been stolen during a national convention on the West Coast. Dr. Dante Simbulan, of the Church Coalition for Human Rights in the Philippines, said that the day after he testified regarding human rights abuses in the Philippines before the House Subcommittee on Asian and Pacific Affairs in June 1983, his house was burglarized. All of these incidents were duly reported to the appropriate U.S. authorities, but none were ever resolved, according to Gillego.[7]

A Freedom of Information Act request revealed that the FBI had accessed the post office box rented by the MFP at the Madison Square Postal Station in Manhattan, which received donations from sympathizers. The *New York Times* reported on a plot to assassinate Manglapus. It had been revealed to him by Eduardo Quintero, a former deputy ambassador to the United States. He identified the would-be assassin as a George Torre, "who told both Quintero and Manglapus that General Ver had offered to drop a murder charge against him in Manila if he agreed to kill Mr. Manglapus. Mr. Torre could not be located." General Fabian Ver was chief of staff of the Philippine Armed Forces and a close associate of Marcos.[8] The *Times* went on to report that "two former high ranking Carter Administration officials said the U.S. interrupted messages from Manila to Philippine agents in this country five years ago ordering them to harass opponents of Mr. Marcos. At the same time, a 1982 (U.S.) Defense Intelligence Agency report made public last week indicated that the Pentagon believed the military attaché to the Philippine Embassy Brig. Gen. Angel G. Kanapi was charged with operating against anti-Marcos dissidents here."

Evidently, the monitoring had started a year after the imposition of martial law. According to a classified 1979 report from the U.S. Senate Committee on Government Operations, "the CIA became aware in October 1973 that the Philippine government had become increasingly concerned that President Marcos's enemies in the U.S. might be developing, or had already, an influence that would adversely affect the Philippine government."[9] Mike Glennon, counsel to the committee, who wrote the report, mentioned three "threat" groups—the MFP; the former mayor of Manila, Antonio Villegas (who never joined any U.S.-based opposition); and Eugenio Lopez, a business tycoon whose assets had been taken over by the government after martial law was imposed, and brother of Marcos's pre–martial law vice president, Fernando Lopez. Marcos was holding Eugenio "Geny" Lopez Jr., Eugenio's son, among his political prisoners, in effect using him as a hostage to keep Eugenio Sr. from agitating against him from the United States. He was also settling a score against the Lopezes. Fernando had turned against him during the last election, using their influential newspaper, the *Manila Chronicle*, and their TV stations to keep up a steady drumbeat of negative news about his administration. Geny was the newspaper's publisher. It was the first newspaper closed down by martial law.

The relationship between Marcos and Lopez Sr. went beyond politics and predated martial law. In a history of oligarchic clans that dominate Philippine life, Alfred McCoy wrote:

> For over thirty years, Lopez had used presidential patronage to secure subsidized government financing and dominate state-regulated industries, thereby amassing the largest private fortune in the Philippines. After declaring martial law in 1972, Marcos used the same state power to demolish the Lopez conglomerates and transfer their assets to a new economic elite of his kin and courtiers . . . During the period of the Philippine Republic (1946–72), the two became master manipulators of the state, operators without peer within their respective realms. Although

Marcos was a career politician and Lopez an entrepreneur, the common commingling of business and politics drew them into the political arena where they met face-to-face, first as allies and later as enemies.[10]

Holding Geny in a military prison cell in Manila was one way that Marcos kept Lopez at bay. Yet even after Geny escaped to the United States in 1977 (as will be described later), Marcos still feared the Lopez clout and reach. Settling in San Francisco, Geny told the *New York Times* in March 1986, before he returned to Manila after Marcos had fled the country, that he operated a small business importing and distributing Filipino foods. He said that his family had spent the last sixteen years selling off bits of real estate. But "every time we tried to embark on some business venture, Mr. Marcos assured that it didn't get off the ground."[11]

The *Washington Post* reported that since 1973, four Filipino agencies had been operating in the United States monitoring anti–martial law groups. Among these were the National Intelligence Security Authority, the National Bureau of Investigation, and the Presidential Security Commission. Marcos had identified the agencies during questioning in Honolulu, where he had fled on February 25, 1986, after being deposed. His testimony was given in connection with a civil suit over the murders of two Filipino labor union activists in Seattle, Washington, who had been known to criticize his regime.[12]

When the extradition threat, the assassination report, the monitoring by agents, and the harassment became widely known, Filipinos were afraid to engage in political activism against the regime. In May 1975, when the MFP publicized the findings of an Amnesty International report accusing the regime of holding 4,553 political prisoners, it was presenting reputable proof that repression was common. But at the same time, the publicity was frightening recruits from their cause. One indication of the spreading fear was the number of Filipinos seeking political asylum. Beginning in July 1980, the Statistical Analysis Branch of the Immigration and Naturalization Service (INS) in Washington, D.C., began classifying asylum applicants by nationality. By September 1983, twenty-one Filipinos had been granted asylum; fifty-nine more had received asylum by June 1985, for a total of eighty cases during a four-and-a-half year period. By ruling in favor of these asylees, the U.S. government was clearly rejecting the regime's assertion that political activists were welcome to return home without fear of imprisonment. Altogether, the INS received 502 asylum applications between July 1980 and April 1984.

One cannot discount the effect of good news circulated by the regime. Multipage glossy advertising inserts in American business magazines such as *Fortune* boasted of an improved climate for business investments and for tourism.[13] The reference to civilian peace was particularly pointed. Various accounts described the Philippines before martial law as a chaotic mess, with rampant violence, crime, and corruption, and with runaway inflation. A month before martial law was imposed, more than a dozen explosions occurred at offices, shopping malls, and government buildings. There was a desperate sense that something drastic had to be done. Hence the early period of calm and civic order imposed by martial law was generally welcomed.

There were some prominent endorsers of the order. Notable among those who considered it justified was General Carlos Romulo, probably the most recognizable Filipino figure among Americans because of his association with General Douglas MacArthur's defeat of Japan during the Pacific War. He waded ashore at Leyte with MacArthur on October 1944 as the general began his campaign to drive out the occupying Japanese forces from the Philippines. For Romulo, the pre–martial law Philippines had become "a wild west country." He considered the surrender of hundreds of thousands of guns the regime's "best achievement," and a necessity for instilling national discipline.[14] In a speech he delivered in San Francisco before the Commonwealth Club of California on May 24, 1973, seven months after martial law had been declared, he presented his case for the validity of its imposition. Not only did the Philippine constitution give the country's chief executive this emergency power, just as President Lincoln had assumed similar powers to save the Union, but it was a necessary move. Democracy, as practiced in accordance with the Philippine model, was "mired in the other darker depths of democracy—the bickering, the factionalism, the corruption, the aimless drift, and more than these, the rebellion of the alienated—the activities of those who would use the façade of democracy to subvert its real meaning and purpose, for their own ends." In essence, he argued, Philippine-style democracy no longer worked. Marcos's "rescue operation" had saved the country from becoming "in effect, a banana republic."[15]

To rebut Romulo's praise of martial law, Manglapus sought an appearance on the widely watched American public affairs program *Meet the Press*. "We have sponsors," he was told. "If you are as well known as Romulo to our sponsors, I might put you on." However, "that was not the case," Manglapus remembered. "So the very fact that Romulo was for Marcos was another one of those things that we had to overcome during our early organizing years."[16]

According to the political scientist David Pacis, it took some time for the disappointment with and resentment of the regime to broaden. He wrote that "generally, throughout the major phases of martial law, Filipinos and international observers accepted Marcos's social contract: clean streets, less crime, and greater purchasing power, among other things, for limited freedoms and fixed elections."[17] On September 1, 1973, the regime launched "Operation Homecoming," inviting all overseas Filipinos, especially those residing in the United States, to visit home between then and February 28, 1974, to see for themselves "the marvelous transformation we have accomplished in the New Society."[18] The returnees were offered reduced airfares, extended visas, tax breaks, and priority immigration and customs service upon arrival at the airport.[19] When Manglapus was asked in an interview with *America* magazine, a Jesuit publication, whether this indicated an openness and confidence on Marcos's part, he replied to the contrary. To his mind, "it indicated a sense of insecurity. Similar homecoming campaigns were subsidized by Hitler and Mussolini for German and Italian Americans in the 1930s as a reaction to hostile feelings among Americans toward their dictatorial methods. . . . Returning Filipinos will see cleaner streets and a surface calm. They will hear nothing of crime or corruption because the media are programmed not to report such matters."[20]

CHAPTER 4

The Big Divide
Differences Hindering Unity

Census studies of Filipino immigration to the U.S. usually describe three "waves" or influxes of arrivals, evoking an image of a relentless, unstoppable mass of immigrants rolling in from the horizon. Another vision conjures boatloads of people, soaking wet, struggling ashore. The first "wave," in truth, came by ship. They were young men hired at the beginning of the twentieth century after the United States acquired the Philippines from Spain in 1898. As America's first colony, the islands provided laborers to work the fields of Hawaii and California. In California, they harvested lettuce and asparagus. Nonagricultural workers performed domestic or personal services, for example, as hotel bellboys, restaurant busboys, or dishwashers. Others worked in factories processing fruits and vegetables, and in Alaska's fish canneries. This period of immigration lasted until 1934, when Filipinos were classified as nationals of an American commonwealth country.

Histories of this period recount high anti-Filipino racial discrimination, especially on the West Coast, by Americans who viewed the newcomers as a threat to their jobs. Most of the Filipinos toiled in low-paying and menial jobs and lived in substandard housing. Their heart-wrenching experiences are described in the anthology *Letters in Exile*.[1] A California Department of Industrial Relations study in 1930 counted 31,092 Filipino immigrants; by 1940, there were 50,000. Most were single males. One study claimed that "official and popular racism prevented the mass of itinerant bachelor farm workers from starting families and producing new generations of U.S.-born Filipinos . . . Filipinos could not bring wives, marry into other races, own property or vote—they were not allowed to become Americans . . . The virtual absence of families precluded the establishment of deeply rooted and enduring communities whose economic, political, and cultural power could grow over time."[2]

In the second "wave," from 1934 to the mid-1960s, Filipinos lost their right of entry as American Commonwealth nationals. Immigration was severely reduced because of legislation that established a quota system based on national origin. Most Filipinos who arrived during this period were nonquota immigrants and temporary visitors, often students. Those who had fought alongside the Americans in liberating the Philippines also qualified as nonquota immigrants. It is estimated that one-third, or four thousand, of the arrivals during this period served with the U.S. armed forces.

The third influx began in 1965, when a new immigration law replaced the quota system. Called the preference system, it set a maximum of twenty thousand immigrants from each non–Western Hemisphere country. The intention of this new legislation was to reunite families. Spouses, minor unmarried children, and parents of U.S. citizens were not counted against the limit. Thus many more than twenty thousand Filipinos actually gained entry.

The new law also awarded immigrant visas to those with particular occupational skills. Thus the gates were opened wide to professionals such as health-care workers, accountants, engineers, teachers, lawyers, and highly skilled technicians. The *Economist*, a London-based weekly, reported that American hospitals were recruiting entire graduating classes of Filipino nurses. A University of the Philippines study concluded that this post-1965 brain drain had a higher monetary value than twenty years' worth of American aid to the Philippines.[3] In one estimate in 1972, a foreign medical doctor was valued at $50,000 when he entered the United States. For other types of professionals, it was $20,000. The INS reported that in 1968, when the new system became fully effective, about 25 percent of all doctors, more than 40 percent of all pharmacists and dentists, and 58 percent of all dietitians who immigrated to the United States came from the Philippines. The professionals had relatively weak ties to people and institutions in the homeland. They wanted higher salaries, better working conditions, and greater professional opportunities not available there.

During the decade between 1960 and 1970, the Filipino population nearly doubled, to 343,000. Two-thirds of that additional population consisted of new immigrants, and that was the segment whose hearts and minds the political exiles struggled mightily to win over. They would soon find out that there was no such thing as a typical Filipino immigrant; as a result, minor and major differences among the newcomers would influence their organizing goals and strategies. In the 1970s, the new immigrants clustered primarily in two places—40 percent of them were in California, and 28 percent in Hawaii—where they joined the majority of earlier immigrants who had come during the first two waves. Between then and 1990, more than 40,000 new immigrants settled in the U.S. each year. Hence, in the span of approximately two decades, the Filipino population swelled to 1.4 million, 300,000 of whom arrived during the Marcos era, between 1972 and 1986. They fanned out from the West Coast to other states—Illinois, New York, New Jersey, Washington, Virginia, Texas, Florida, and Maryland. During this period, more immigrants came from the Philippines than from any other country except Mexico. They constituted the largest among the Asian groups, more numerous than the Chinese and the Japanese. As a result, the exiles faced an ever-expanding challenge: reaching out to a far more dispersed, and more numerous, group. Add to their numbers the Filipinos who entered as nonimmigrants, estimated by the INS at more than 400,000 visitors each year between 1965 and 1974. They brought with them their own perceptions of martial law back home that they communicated to the immigrants.[4]

The 1965 wave brought distinctive historical experiences with them, too. As white-collar workers, fluent in English and attuned to American culture (having lived through fifty years of American tutelage after the end of the war in 1945), they easily adapted to their new home. With those advantages, they did not have to settle into ethnic enclaves in U.S. cities as other Asian immigrants did. "They arrive in America capable of reading supermarket labels, dealing with American tradesmen and joining in America's pop culture," wrote the *Economist*.[5] But by preferring white-collar jobs to ethnic-based commerce, it added, they cut themselves off from a way of rising in society that had helped other Asians boost their average earnings above those of white Americans. Their first order of business was to put in place the basic necessities—employment, housing, and education for their children. There was no time or inclination to indulge in political activities. And anyway, they had left the homeland for good—the future was now America, and making it there.

On the whole, they made it. In California, 42 percent were employed as clerical and sales workers, while 21 percent were professionals. In other states, 55 percent worked as professionals. This percentage tripled between

1960 and 1980. In the 1980s, Filipinos earned 18 percent less on average than Japanese and 13 percent less than Chinese or whites, but 18 percent more than Hispanics and blacks. Yet they had the second-lowest rate of family poverty after the Japanese because more Filipino women worked outside the home.[6]

However, the younger, newest segment of this wave, mostly students—single, undecided about where to put down roots, and perhaps with plans to return home after completing their degrees—chose to maintain their ties to the Philippines. The Filipino exiles found this segment of the immigrant population to be more receptive and responsive to their organizing efforts. University student groups were the audience for early public speaking appearances. They came to meetings. They marched and chanted and hoisted placards at street demonstrations in front of Philippine consulates. But their numbers were small in comparison to the much larger group of apathetic, unconcerned, fearful immigrants.

Having made it, the latter centered their community involvement on social and fraternal groups. They formed Philippine regional, professional, and school alumni associations with others who shared their interests. Many promoted projects to raise money, via fundraising balls and donations, to send back to their former towns and schools. Very few, if any, of these groups were openly political associations organized to promote the platforms of the two major American political parties. Wary of any attempt to link their associations with the exile groups, they refused to invite exile speakers as guest speakers to their social functions. Indeed, rank-and-file members protested when their leaders did so.

Political awareness was rarely their hallmark. Although the proportion of naturalized citizens was larger among Filipinos than among other Asian groups, their turnout for U.S. general elections was low. Most of the 45 percent of Filipinos who did vote during the 2008 U.S. presidential election were registered as Democrats, in contrast to other Southeast Asians, who were more evenly split, with 36 percent voting Republican and 34 percent voting Democratic.[7]

A study of the role of media in the life of Filipino immigrants during the martial law years concluded that by 1982, certain demographics divided the population:

> What exists is a dichotomy within the overall group, and it is produced by several factors. One is demographical, a large West coast population and a smaller East coast population. Another is the amount of time in

the United States, the West coast population being much older. A third factor are the educational levels, the East coast having a higher educational attainment. A fourth is financial security and well-being, the East coast exhibiting a higher standard of living and a greater potential for development. Finally, while not strictly related to demographics, is the political dichotomy: after 1972 the Filipino-American group split into pro and opposing Marcos factions. Most of the opposition groups were based in California. This is perhaps not surprising given the economic situation of this Western group and their historical tradition of political activism (this group was integral in the formation of the early California labor unions). The Eastern group, perhaps on account of their rapid social advancement, showed a smaller amount of political activism; professional conservatism or political ambivalence concerning the Marcos government seems to be the norm.[8]

In addition to these geographic, educational, and income differences, there was a generational divide. The second wave of immigrants, commonly referred to as "old-timers" (an accurate characterization, since many of them had arrived in the early part of the twentieth century as farmworkers), had lived in the United States for so long that most had lost touch with and interest in the homeland. In contrast, the third wave consisted primarily of a youthful generation who had experienced the fervent anti-Marcos student activism that had roiled Manila's streets and universities even before martial law. The most active among them formed the core of the "leftist" U.S. anti–martial law groups, first and foremost among which was the Katipunan Ng Mga Demokratikong Pilipino (KDP), based in Oakland, California. The KDP viewed the "centrist" MFP exile leadership as representative of an oligarchic class that was partly responsible for the problems in the homeland. Hence a class as well as an ideological divide complicated the dynamics of a population that the exiles sought to win over to their side.

Other observers pointed to the regional and linguistic origins of the immigrants. Stereotypes and prejudices were common among the northern Ilocanos, the southern Visayans, and the central Tagalogs—the three main Philippine language and provincial groups. To various degrees, this colored their political views. For example, Marcos was an Ilocano, so it was no surprise that he remained the beloved son among Ilocano Filipino immigrants throughout the martial law years. As James P. Allen of California State University noted:

Thus the [Filipino] immigrants have created not just one but a set of ethnic subsocieties. These subsocieties form a fluid rather than a rigid structure, but some do have distinguishing locational characteristics. With differences based on region of origin and social distinctions between those who received their academic training in the United States and those trained in the Philippines, between the college educated and the kitchen and cannery workers, between the old, single farm workers and the young navy recruits, between activist students and those who are comfortably established, it is evident that the social structure and spatial patterns of the American people are being elaborated in no simple way.[9]

Because it was difficult to bridge these divides, the exile opposition faced a number of organizing challenges. Over the span of the three immigration waves, no one unifying, encompassing issue had galvanized Filipinos in the United States. True, the fight against racial discrimination had brought them together with other Asians, as well as blacks and Hispanics, to take part in nationwide campaigns. But as a single issue that consumed only Filipinos, nothing has surpassed the imposition of martial law. The appeal of issues such as the licensing of foreign-trained professionals (doctors, pharmacists, dentists) and, more recently, the awarding of World War II benefits to Filipino veterans who fought with the Americans in the Philippines was much too narrow to unify the fragmented communities. Martial law, on the other hand, affected everyone, in that it touched family and friends back home. And as Marcos functionaries mounted campaigns to win over Filipinos in the U.S., they had to reach out far and wide. On their heels, the exile opposition targeted the very same audiences. There were no divides in this contest to win hearts and minds.

CHAPTER 5

Martial Law and Beyond

How the Dictator Usurped Power

At this inaugural address as the sixth president of the Philippine Republic on December 30, 1965, at Luneta Park in Manila, Ferdinand Marcos proclaimed: "We must rise from the depths of ignominy and failure. Our government is gripped in the iron hand of venality, its treasury is barren, its resources are wasted, its civil service is slothful and indifferent, its armed forces demoralized and its councils sterile." His election, he stated, "is a new mandate of leadership. It is . . . a mandate not merely for change. It is a mandate for greatness . . . Come then, let us march together towards the dream of greatness."[1]

In the same speech, he invoked the nation's overthrow of three hundred years of Spanish colonial rule that began in 1521, and the establishment of the first republic in Asia in 1898. Left unsaid was that the republic was short-lived. Some months earlier, the United States had declared war on Spain, ostensibly for blowing up an American ship in Cuba, a Spanish colony. Admiral George Dewey of the U.S. Navy steamed into Manila Bay and sank the Spanish flotilla. Rather than surrender to the Filipinos, who had virtually vanquished them before Dewey arrived, the Spaniards ceded the islands to the Americans in a simulated handover. In the same year, the United States annexed Guam, Puerto Rico, and Hawaii, its first steps toward empire. Betrayed and unwilling to serve another master, the Filipinos waged a five-year losing battle that killed 216,000 inhabitants (out of a population of 7.4 million) and 4,234 American troops (out of 126,458 invading forces).[2] For fifty years, the islands were America's first overseas colony. They fell to Japan in World War II and were liberated after great loss of lives and property. When the war ended, only in Warsaw was the devastation greater than in Manila.

The Philippines gained its sovereignty from the United States in 1946. It was during the term of the country's first president, Manuel Roxas (1946–48), that a series of trade and military agreements sealed a long association of "mutual interests" between the two countries. Under one of those agreements, the Philippines leased two military bases on the island of Luzon to the United States for a term of ninety-nine years. These ties bound the two countries to an overarching relationship of economics and security that would span succeeding administrations.

When Marcos was elected president in 1965, an insurgency by the leftist New People's Army (NPA) and a secessionist Muslim movement in the south were brewing. The Communist leanings of the NPA worried the United States, which was already mired in a war in Indochina. It viewed the Philippines as a vital defense line in the Cold War with the Soviet Union. Keeping the islands within its sphere of influence at a time when Communism was threatening the rest of Southeast Asia constituted a core national interest. The powerful linkages—of politics, trade, and military and foreign aid—that it had forged during the colonial, commonwealth, and post-independence eras were at stake.

Relationships were being nurtured at high levels. The U.S. vice president, Hubert Humphrey, attended Marcos's inauguration. In September 1966, Marcos met with President Lyndon Johnson in Washington to sign a $45 million economic aid package and to negotiate a new twenty-five-year lease term for the bases. The next month Johnson visited Manila for a seven-nation conference to rally support among Asian allies for the United States' war in Vietnam. Despite a public outcry against the idea of getting involved, Marcos sent an engineering battalion to South Vietnam. It was later revealed at a hearing on November 18 before the U.S. Senate Committee on Foreign Relations that the United States had secretly paid $39 million to persuade Marcos to dispatch ten battalions.[3]

Marcos's dream of a march to greatness started well. Expansive public works projects as well as intensified tax collection led to a measure of prosperity in the 1970s. He was reelected in 1969, becoming the first president to win a second term. President Richard Nixon visited that year, followed by the governor of California, Ronald Reagan, beginning a friendship that would blossom during Reagan's subsequent presidency.[4]

During Marcos's second term, militancy increased among student groups. Kabataang Makabayan (Nationalist Youth), the most militant of all, allied itself with the new Communist Party of the Philippines, founded on December 26, 1968. In February and March 1970, youths marched against the U.S. embassy in Manila. In April, following three days of rioting, a general strike was launched to protest increased oil and transportation costs. In one street demonstration after another, students demanded Marcos's resignation. To compound the heightening civil instability, a deranged man attempted to assassinate Pope Paul VI upon his arrival in Manila on November 27 for a three-day visit.

There were two major events on the calendar amid this climate of unrest—congressional elections and a convention held to replace the 1935 Philippine constitution, written during the American colonial period. At a pre-election rally by the opposition Liberal Party in Manila's Plaza Miranda on August 21, 1971, grenades exploded. Twelve people were killed and about one hundred wounded, among them notable party candidates. Marcos charged Communist terrorists with plotting to overthrow the government and vowed to impose martial law. Bloody violence marked the November 7 elections, in which the Liberals won six of the eight contested Senate seats. Only two of Marcos's party candidates won.

On July 7, 1972, the convention voted to change the form of government from presidential rule to a parliamentary system. This allowed Marcos, whose last and second term would have ended in December 1973, to seek a third term. Manglapus had been elected a delegate to the convention and together with several colleagues had campaigned against the resolution allowing a third term. The press revealed that Imelda Marcos, the president's wife, was distributing envelopes containing money to key delegates as a bribe to get them to pass the resolution.

On September 22, Marcos signed the martial law decree, which was dated September 21. As justification, he claimed that an "armed insurrection and rebellion" was being waged against the government by "lawless elements" and "terroristic organizations."[5] (There had been two explosions at a Manila electric company on September 11, and there was an alleged assassination attempt on Defense Minister Juan Ponce Enrile on September 22 that was used to further justify his decree.) He would wield absolute power for the next fourteen years and eight months.

A multitude of reasons have been advanced for why his rule lasted for so long. He was a brilliant tactician; he outwitted his political enemies; he cut off the economic base of the oligarchs and fostered "crony capitalism"; he appointed generals from his Ilocos region and made the military establishment his own police force; he kept the United States on his side, ensuring the flow of economic and military aid; he imprisoned his most outspoken critics and political rivals. At the time, the local opposition was weak, disorganized, and ineffective. And in shuttering the Philippine Congress and its lawmaking process by issuing decrees and proclamations in its place, he resorted to a series of legalistic maneuvers to provide a semblance of a democratic process. The new constitution was ratified not by a plebiscite-style direct vote of the people, but by a voice vote of so-called citizens' assemblies.

On July 23, 1973, Marcos conducted a referendum to ascertain whether the electorate wanted him to continue serving beyond his term so that he could complete his martial law reforms. According to official figures, 96.7 percent of the 18 million voters said yes. On February 27, 1975, he asked voters whether they approved of the manner by which he issued decrees and proclamations with the force of law, and whether they wanted him to continue exercising such powers. According to the official count, close to 89 percent of the 82 million voters agreed. Imelda Marcos was named the governor of Metro Manila. And in yet another referendum, on October 16, 1976, several amendments to the new constitution were approved, allowing Marcos to exercise his powers until martial law was lifted and giving him emergency legislative powers when the National Assembly was not in session or when he deemed it necessary. The next step would be to consolidate his power over a national assembly called the Interim Batasang Pambansa (IBP). Pre–martial law political parties were invited to field candidates for the 1978 elections for seats against his newly organized party, Kilusang Bagong Lipunan (KBL—the New Society Movement). The Liberal Party boycotted the elections. The Lakas Ng Bayan (LABAN—People Power) was headed by Senator Benigno Aquino, a Marcos critic, who campaigned from his jail cell. The KBL took 187 seats against 13 candidates from the opposition. In Manila, it won all 21 seats, crushing LABAN. Marcos named his wife minister of human settlements, a new office.

The U.S. press mocked the conduct of the elections. The *New York Times* said that refusing to grant the imprisoned Aquino a temporary release to campaign on the grounds of endangering national security was not credible. "If Mr. Marcos believes his own claims, he should have nothing to fear from letting Mr. Aquino campaign." The *Washington Post* described the election as "phony . . . His wife Imelda, unleashed extra dollops of her formidable patronage and charm."[6]

At the January 1980 elections for governors and mayors, the first under martial law, KBL candidates won 69 of 73 gubernatorial positions and 1,450 of 1,560 mayoral posts. The Liberal Party and LABAN boycotted the elections. By the sixth year of martial law, Marcos's regime was firmly entrenched nationwide.

This series of political events is described here because the exile oppositionists orchestrated their campaigns in the United States to respond to each event in coordination with their Philippine allies. These campaigns would take the form of letter writing to the U.S. Congress and the media, street demonstrations, chapter meetings, and community outreach protests.

CHAPTER 6

Early Organizing

Conflicting Opposition Groups

The exile opposition found itself reacting to Marcos's every move rather than taking the offensive. Manila's pro-government newspapers labeled the groups as feeble as their Philippine counterparts, thundering against farcical referendum and sham election exercises—to no avail. When the exiles first began to mount an opposition front, they had no idea that Marcos's staying power would test their endurance and commitment. Within a year after the September 1972 imposition of martial law, enough members and a core of leaders got together to formally create identifiable groups—the MFP was established at a convention in Washington, D.C., on September 22, 1973, and the Friends of the Filipino People (FFP) on October 20, 1973, in Philadelphia. The Katipunan Ng Mga Demokratikong Pilipino (KDP; Union of Democratic Filipinos) is said to have had its beginnings in California in August 1973.[1]

In the following years, splits and mergers among and between these groups created a succession of other subgroups, all offshoots of these pioneers. Early on, the MFP was tagged by its members and the American media as "moderate" or "centrist." It appealed "to the more conservative and well-to-do elements of the Philippine community in the United States," said Daniel Boone Schirmer, a historian of Philippine-U.S. relations and a founding member of the FFP. According to Schirmer, "it had become clear that the U.S. government was supporting the Marcos dictatorship, and . . . the job of ending Washington's support . . . could not be left to the democratic-minded members of the Philippine community in the United States, but would have to be shouldered as well, and especially, by members of the non-Filipino majority."[2] Hence most of the sixty attendees at its 1973 founding, who came from New York, Philadelphia, Washington, Connecticut, and Massachusetts, were Americans. The FFP maintained a lobbyist, the Filipina lawyer Severina Rivera, in Washington, D.C.

"Boone was adamant that FFP should not attempt to advocate for a particular type of political alternative to the Marcos dictatorship such as KDP and MFP which addressed a Filipino constituency," said Barbara Gaerlan, another FFP founder. "Rather Boone insisted that FFP should have two guiding principles: opposition to U.S. governmental support for dictatorship in the Philippines, and opposition to the U.S. military bases in the Philippines which effectively propped up the dictatorship, in addition to making the world less stable because of military expansion. He stressed that Filipinos should decide their own political destiny and that the U.S. should keep hands off."[3]

Gaerlan traces the FFP's informal beginnings in 1972 to "a small collective of anti-Marcos Filipinos" in New York City who were publishing a magazine for non-Filipinos in the United States about the situation in the Philippines. Titled the *Philippines Information Bulletin*, it "cavalierly included in the masthead the statement that PIB was published by 'American Friends of the Filipino People,' even though no such group actually existed. Because they were worried about Marcos reprisals, most of the names of authors and other people used in the magazine were also pseudonyms." When the FFP formally organized in 1973, Gaerlan said: "it would be a good idea if the magazine could emerge from the murky underground of pseudonyms and be handed over to people who actually were American friends of the Filipino people."[4] Eventually the word "American" was dropped.

The KDP grew out of a 1972 organization called the National Committee for the Restoration of Civil Liberties in the Philippines (NCRCLP). It was based in San Francisco, and according to Rodel Rodis, one of its founders, it came into being on September 21, 1972, on the same weekend that martial law was declared in Manila. Rodis said that by October 6 it had formed protest pickets in front of Philippine consulates. Many of the NCRCLP members had been active in the militant student movements in the Philippines before martial law. As a result, the KDP was viewed as the radical element among the exile opposition. In December 1974, an Anti–Martial Law Coalition (AMLC) was formed in a move to coordinate the work of the FFP and KDP. The next year, the coalition was renamed the Philippine Solidarity Network/Congress Task Force.

Rene Cruz, a KDP founding member, dates the actual birth of the group to July 1973 in Santa Cruz, California. He said that Filipino "radicals" from all over the U.S. met, then took on "the task of uniting a ragtag group of close to 200 activists," led by "a nine-member National Council."[5] The core members, in addition to Cruz, were Bruce Ocena, Melinda Paras, and Cynthia Maglaya. The coalition focused its efforts on exposing the United States' maintenance of bases in the Philippines as the root cause of American intervention in Philippine affairs. Philippine-based oppositionists endorsed the same position. In 1978, Philippine senator Jose Diokno collected signatures calling for the removal of the bases and sent the statement to the FFP for publication in national newspapers. Several thousand dollars were raised to pay for the ads. Schirmer described what happened next:

> At this time, the FFP had a national staff of four whose duty it was to implement the policies of the National Committee. Three of the staff were members of the KDP. In April 1979, a meeting of the National Committee of the FFP took place and we inquired about the ad. We were told by KDP members of the staff that it would be politically incorrect to give publicity to the Manila statement. The reason, they said, was that it was signed by Senator Benigno Aquino and Aquino was well known to have worked with the CIA in the Philippines. Therefore the whole statement was suspect and Diokno and the others might be nothing more than unwitting dupes of the CIA. We were led to understand that this was the analysis of the national leadership of the KDP. When Senator Diokno was later told the story, he laughed and said that he had worked hard to get Aquino's signature and had considered it quite a triumph when he succeeded.[6]

When asked to expand on the KDP's analysis, Schirmer said: "To have asserted that the CIA in any way promoted a broadly signed statement of Philippine opposition to the bases was to be guilty of a non sequitur, quite contrary to the reality of the case. The fact is Aquino signed the statement despite his tendency to lean towards U.S. policy objectives. His signature therefore helped give the support of the statement its unusual breadth and was especially pleasing to those consistent nationalists like Senator Diokno who originated it."[7]

Schirmer believed that the bases statement that ultimately caused the FFP to part ways with the KDP was emblematic of a more serious flaw with the latter organization. He said, "first of all . . . , the KDP leaders considered themselves so acute politically that they took upon themselves what they thought of as a vanguard role so that all their policies were to be carried out by the members of their organization more or less as commands, whatever the cost. And in this case the cost was the democratic life of the FFP as an organization. Secondly, their off-the-wall assessment of the 1978 Philippine anti-bases statement could only have resulted from an ultra-left cast of thought."[8]

In a June 1996 interview, Therese Rodriguez, a KDP leader, said, "the main split between KDP and FFP was how do you undertake lobbying work in Washington at a time when what was very clear was that Marcos was being supported by the U.S. Cut off aid or maintain the grassroots to gain influence? Not just cut a few millions but to cut all aid and that meant build up grassroots support." She added that in the early stages of organizing by the various opposition groups, it was necessary to establish "ideological and political differences in order to distinguish each other more clearly. And also, we were really trying to figure out the alternative to the Philippine political system. There was no consensus. After Marcos, what? That was the political reality that confronted us and as we took on the responsibility of educating the community, we tended to borrow a lot from our ideological perspective."[9]

Amado David, another KDP leader, admitted that "KDP was to the left. It was that way for a reason. It was a very disciplined organization. It had a line close to the communist National Democratic Front [NDF] in the Philippines. I believed we needed that kind of organization to create a national organization here. We moved where the work was to be done, from city to city. There was no email at that time. We had no fax machines. We handed out press releases by hand. The work was very labor intensive . . . handing out leaflets at churches, to Filipino parishioners."[10] He said that the KDP had a core membership of two hundred nationwide.

The KDP acknowledged that no one in their leadership ranks had the established reputation of Manglapus, which was one reason why members were drawn to the MFP. "The media only paid attention to Manglapus," said Rodriguez. "It was not a good thing because the media was not hearing the other side of the spectrum. But then we realized that the constant attention to and the consistency of Manglapus in his political position is very important and should be supported. We could not do anything about the reality that we were not a former senator."[11]

The left broke up as well when not everyone was willing to toe the NDF "line." The rift occurred during the February 1986 presidential elections pitting Marcos against Corazon (Cory) Aquino, the widow of Benigno.

One KDP group followed the NDF call for a boycott, mocking it as a fraudulent exercise. They believed that with the United States behind Marcos, he would not lose. Another KDP group urged all opposition forces to unite behind Mrs. Aquino, sensing that the people, who were outraged at the murder of her husband, would unseat Marcos through the electoral process. Before this rift, the KDP was also riven by internal disputes about its goals in the Filipino communities. It pursued what it called a "dual program": supporting its NDF allies in the Philippines against Marcos and doing grassroots "socialist" work in Filipino communities. This took the form of promoting the KDP as the "vanguard" in fighting against racial discrimination and for labor rights, better housing, immigrant rights, and the like. In both programs, "the U.S. was seen as the primary instigator of the racist and imperialist policies that maintained Filipino racial and national oppression in the U.S. and the Philippines."[12]

A KDP chapter in Chicago was expected to leaflet Filipino parishioners early in the morning at a church and at the same time build support groups for two Filipino nurses accused of killing their patients at a veterans' hospital there. Members debated constantly on which activity should take priority—the Filipinos at home or the Filipinos in the United States? They could not pursue two simultaneous "revolutions."[13] Consequently the Chicago chapter split up, "but after intense discussions over differences the chapter was reintegrated—with the dual program intact."[14]

Because of the KDP's radical reputation, the MFP was wary about working too closely with it and its leftist allies. It had to contend with a conservative U.S. Congress suspicious of lobbyists with leftist ties who were espousing total withdrawal of aid, both military and economic, a stand that the MFP considered unrealistic. In a lobbying trip to Washington in 1985, during which Manglapus was scheduled to meet with some members of Congress and their aides, he said that the session "comes at a propitious time when we are fighting the 'either Marcos or the Communists' syndrome articulated by Reagan. As usual the extreme left are trying to get into the act on this one and we are doing our best to keep them from infiltrating in order not to waste this opportunity of making a clear distinction between us and them. The need for this distinction may not be as evident outside Washington. And I can understand the pressures for joint action."[15]

The MFP had a more unautocratic, nonjudgmental attitude toward the political and ideological inclinations of the members it accepted. Everybody was welcome so long as they subscribed to a nonviolent process of dismantling martial law. Nonetheless, friction built up between the leaders, some of whom pushed for a closer alliance with the Philippine and Filipino American left. As a result, one group was actively involved in "destabilization" bombing activities in Manila, while another denied having any knowledge of it. The MFP also split in the 1980s when a leading officer formed the Ninoy Aquino Movement, siphoning membership from the MFP.

Bonifacio Gillego, director of the MFP's Philippine Affairs Office, was the group's strongest advocate for closer relations with the Filipino left, both in the homeland and in the United States. He argued that until the diffuse, fragmented non-Communist forces in the Philippines were able to unite, it was "necessary and desirable" for them to ally with the left.[16] The latter had a disciplined party (the Communist Party of the Philippines), an army (the New People's Army), and a political arm (the National Democratic Front). The KDP, its Communist ally in the United States, aware of Gillego's stand, depended on him to mobilize MFP manpower in communal activities with them. On the occasion of the MFP's executive council meeting in Toronto on July 6, 1985, Gillego presented his alliance proposal. "As the Council members are of disparate political orientation, decision on the proposal was held in abeyance. It should be clear, however, that the [proposal] reflects my personal views, not necessarily those of the MFP as an organization," he said.[17]

Organizational conflicts and breakups were common among exile political activists. What mattered was that they stayed focused on their primary goals. The first item on their agendas was to make the American public aware of the emergence of organized U.S.-based resistance. This had to be done quickly, while the Philippines was grabbing international headlines in the early 1970s. In the case of the MFP, as soon as Manglapus's family escaped, he went on a speaking blitz that targeted a wide range of listeners—from college students to policy makers. Invitations to speak before associations whose members included influential opinion makers in foreign policy were highly valued. A sampling of his 1973 appearances includes the Asia Society in Washington, D.C. (June); the National Congress of Christian Democrats in Rome (June); the University of Hawaii (July); the Canadian Institute of International Affairs in Ontario (July); the Commonwealth Club of California in San Francisco (August); the World Affairs Council of Northern California in San Francisco (August); Yale University (September); the State University of New York at Brockport (October); and the University of Rochester (October). As a former foreign minister, he projected the movement's agenda to people who could sway foreign policy toward the Philippines. And as a founder of the Christian Social Movement Party in his country, he had ties to Christian Democrats in Europe and Latin America that brought him worldwide publicity.

Because Manglapus was the first Filipino exile with name recognition from an established reputation in the Philippines, coupled with the fact that no other political personality of the same stature was speaking openly, Filipino organizations such as the Barangay Association of America, the Katbalogan-On Association, and the Filipino Coast Guards in Brooklyn invited him to deliver the keynote address at their social events. These speaking appearances served as a springboard for the formation of local chapters. Organizers were encouraged to publicize the event, distribute information materials, raise funds, and recruit members. By August 1974, the MFP had established chapters in California, Connecticut, Hawaii, Illinois, Michigan, New Jersey, and New York.

The non-MFP groups were basically social networks of regional, hometown, occupational, or school associations. Before the emergence of openly political groups such as the MFP and the KDP, these associations disavowed any partisan involvement in politics, whether U.S. or Philippine in origin. Their inaugural balls and fundraising events highlighted festivity, not political issues that members regarded as divisive. Hence it would take some nerve for the leader of an association to invite an openly political figure to be its guest speaker. Here is an account of one such event in 1976 published in *Washington Magazine*:

> The scene in the ballroom of the Holiday Inn in Independence, Ohio, was festive. It was a warm midsummer evening and the members of the Dulag Circle USA, Inc., a Filipino social club, were in a partying mood. Hula girls and a folk dance troupe were ready to go. Everybody had just finished a good dinner.
>
> Before the beginning of the festivities however, some serious business was in order. Raul Manglapus, former foreign minister and senator of the Philippines and leader of the Filipino exile movement in this country, was scheduled to speak.
>
> At the conclusion of the speech, Ernie Abrograr, an officer of the club, who happens to favor President Ferdinand Marcos, the Filipino strongman, took the podium.
>
> "We thank Professor Manglapus for his remarks but must point out that the opinions expressed by him do not represent the opinions of the

Dulag Circle." A few people clapped. Then Dr. Pete Anloague, the master of ceremonies, came to the microphone.

"Before we get any further," he began, "let me say that the opinion expressed by the speaker who has just preceded me does NOT represent the opinions of this club." The audience burst into long and sustained applause and the party was underway.[18]

Manglapus's meetings across the country with members of the Filipino immigrant community inspired local interest in organizing MFP chapters. By 1979, there were seventy-nine U.S. chapters. Liaison offices were established in Canada (five sites), Australia, France, Italy, Japan, and Saudi Arabia.[19]

When Manglapus spoke at the University of New Orleans in 1978, he found himself in the state where historians say that Filipinos established their first permanent settlement in North America in 1763. They were descendants of Filipinos brought by the Spaniards from Manila on their way back to Spain during the galleon trade years, 1556–1813. Fewer than a thousand Filipinos were living in New Orleans when Manglapus arrived, but the Philippine government maintained a consulate there to serve Filipinos in the southwest region of the United States. In the same location were a consulate charged with upholding the regime and a small MFP opposition group, illustrative of the sparring that took place once a chapter was born. "There were 20 to 25 of us who were the most active," recalled Cipriano and Marina Espina, the MFP chairpersons. "About 125 came to Raul's speech, mostly curious Americans. During demonstrations in front of the consulate, they taunted us—'Why don't you go home?' We shot back: 'If you like Marcos so much, why don't YOU go home?' They wrote letters to the local newspapers praising Marcos. We rebutted. When we called some doctors to come to our meetings, they were mad. 'Don't ever call us again. We are not political.' A lot of problems in organizing. There was heightened surveillance after our MFP 1979 convention when we dropped our no violence policy. We were ostracized by the Filipino community. Local officials were sympathetic. Contributions were sent anonymously."[20]

One technique that the exiles employed to draw public attention (and thereby media publicity) was to stage protest events that overlapped with political developments in the Philippines. These demonstrations, seminars, church masses, and memorial observances not only generated local attention, they also signaled solidarity with the opposition events in Manila. For example, the individual exile groups set aside their differences to demonstrate against the various referenda and elections. Masses for political prisoners on hunger strikes were scheduled at churches with large numbers of Filipino parishioners. One of the earliest and largest street demonstrations was a raucous gathering in New York City on November 14, 1974, in front of the entrance to the Philippine consulate on Fifth Avenue in Manhattan. A press corps from Manila attended, and their dispatches must have made it clear that the freedom of assembly was alive and well in the United States but forbidden in Manila. After Aquino's death, the exiles organized religious observances on every anniversary of his assassination.

Philippine Independence Day rallies (June 12) became a regular occasion for communal activity. Because there were only a few of these staged events over the course of a year, the exiles exploited each one to the hilt. When busloads of MFP members traveled to Washington, D.C., to lobby, they would hand out leaflets. One side detailed the amount of U.S. military aid being given to the Philippines; the other side listed the names of political prisoners and described in graphic detail the torture they suffered. People would literally stop in their tracks upon reading them, and they were then urged to contact their members of Congress. A secretariat based in New York City produced pamphlets and booklets, coordinated mailings to Congress, and distributed media clippings, press releases, and copies of Manglapus's speeches. A newsletter provided updates on foreign aid appropriations, alerting members when to send letters to their congressional representatives. Printed materials from the "underground press" in the Philippines exposing abuses of martial law were especially valued and were widely distributed to members of Congress and the U.S. media.

The FFP and the KDP pursued similar activities. When a major Philippine event, such as a referendum or an election, was scheduled, the major groups would stage simultaneous street demonstrations outside Philippine consulates across the country. The Philippine government could not compete with the constant drumbeat of negative publicity from the U.S. media. In 1975, Manila's secretary of information, Francisco Tatad, expressed his dismay that "neither the American press nor the American Congress seems to have been spared the barrage of anti-Philippine propaganda, which seems to have had the effect of misleading otherwise well-meaning American individuals."[21]

In 1989 in Hawaii, where he had fled after being deposed in 1986, Marcos himself acknowledged that the exile information campaign had been effective, arguing that "the primary reason for the shift in the once-friendly U.S. posture toward his regime was the 'contrived image of Philippine reality' implanted in the U.S. public opinion during the 1970s and the early 1980s 'by the articulate and well-financed representatives of anti-Marcos expatriates residing in North America.'" He added that "the representation made by anti-Marcos spokesmen in committee and subcommittee hearings in the United States Congress were given the widest circulation by the American press; [and that] the wildest charges [against him] were given credence."[22] In 1980, when Senator Aquino was allowed to travel to the United States on condition that he would not speak against Marcos, he hit the speaking circuit as soon as he was able. "A pact with the devil is no pact," he remarked. In November and December, he spoke at Brandeis University, Ohio State University, the Council on Foreign Relations, the Secretary's Forum at the U.S. State Department, and the Asia Society in New York.

An important U.S.-based ally was the Church Coalition for Human Rights in the Philippines. Composed of Catholic and Protestant clergy leaders with ties to their Philippine colleagues, and with an organized base in American communities, they marshaled their considerable influence to protest human rights violations. It was not politics but "moral and humanitarian concerns" that motivated them. According to Schirmer, the Church Coalition decided "to organize themselves separately so as to direct and concentrate their work of education in the ranks of religious and church-going people."[23] The work of FFP members and the Church Coalition carried more weight than the voices of nonvoting Filipino residents. Recognizing their influence, Philippine spokesmen warned them that they were being suckered by the exile groups. They derided MFP leaders as "steak commandos" living off American generosity in comfort and branded KDP members as anti-God Communists.

Teodoro "Doroy" Valencia, a fervent advocate of martial law and a widely read columnist for the *Bulletin Today*, a Manila-based newspaper, compared the exiles to "real rebels in the hills of the Philippines . . . suffering in hotels and eating steak, having fun in moviehouses and meetings. The leadership of the rebels in the USA are people who can't take the discipline of the New Society nor the privation in the Sierra Madre [mountains of the NPA rebels]."[24] He leveled the same charge at the signers of a large ad in the *New York Times* in May 1974 headlined "Americans Concerned for the Philippines." He implied that the signers were Communist dupes, representing the far left of America's liberals. A number of the signers happened to be members of the clergy. On the first anniversary of martial law, the government invited exile leaders to return home in order to see for themselves the improvements the regime had made. The oppositionists never took seriously the assurance that no harm would befall them during their stay.

The MFP's financial resources were always meager. For a year the organization had no physical office, only a Manhattan post office box. When its first secretary-general, J. Pete Fuentecilla, handed over a certified check to pay for an ad in the *New York Times* announcing the formation of the organization, he "could see from the face of the clerk that he had no trust in political movements," he remembered. "And when he took the check, that pretty much depleted the treasury of our new Finance Committee."[25]

Although as many as five hundred people attended Manglapus's speaking appearances, only a fraction of the target Filipino population (approximately one thousand people) were active MFP members. Fear and apathy continued to prevail. In September 1975, MFP teams spent four weekends collating, folding, stuffing, and mailing solicitations for a clandestine radio station to be based offshore from the Philippines. The mailing list contained about eight thousand names of Filipino physicians practicing in the United States. Only sixty responded.

In 1972, the year martial law was imposed, there were 8,846 Filipino medical graduates in the United States, meaning that one out of every eight non-U.S.-born foreign doctors (a full 17.8 percent of all foreign-trained doctors) was from the Philippines. Their numbers had increased fourfold after the 1965 preference system increased the quota for professional immigrants.[26] They were also young: 76 percent were under forty years of age (compared to 47 percent for all other foreign-born doctors). While they were widely dispersed across the country, many of the first immigrant doctors settled in Illinois. They represented a highly desirable segment for the opposition to recruit as members. Quick to establish themselves economically, they had disposable income to spare for donations.

The nature of their work, their extensive social connections, and their high standing in Filipino communities gave them the base for leadership posts. Three doctors were named to the first set of MFP officers. They also provided much-needed seed money. Later chapters were led by doctors, notable among whom were Dr. Ruben Mallari and Dr. Cesar Candari (California); Dr. Philip Chua (Indiana); Dr. Jojo Villalon (Illinois); Dr. Arturo Taca, Dr. Julieta Orbeta, Dr. Augusto Climaco, and Dr. Enrico Farinas (Missouri); Dr. Orlando Apiado (New York); Dr. Ben Malabanan (Texas); and Dr. Arturo Monteiro (Washington, D.C.).

The martial law government was equally desirous of winning the Filipino doctors to its side. The Association of Philippine Practicing Physicians (APPA), formed in 1973, and its three thousand members served as one arena. For a decade, Dr. Taca, the head of the St. Louis chapter, chided the association's members and leaders to drop their nominally nonpolitical partisanship and speak openly against the martial law regime. "Although the APPA started innocuously as a professional organization," he wrote in his memoir, "partisan lines were already being drawn between the Marcos supporters and a sprinkling of members who were against the dictatorship. Sadly, the anti-Marcos personalities, not only outnumbered, were also quite timid . . . When I joined the APPA the Marcos hirelings had the whole field to themselves with absolutely no opposition."[27] Taca did not mince words in describing his feelings about them, calling them "fascistic," "elitist," "a sorry lot," "plainly disgusting," and "reprehensible."

CHAPTER 7

Learning How to Lobby

How the United States Fought the Exiles

As soon as the MFP had established its structure, it launched its first lobbying campaign, against the Foreign Assistance Act of 1973. Each year a bill to allocate and authorize funding for foreign assistance projects underwent an approval process in the two chambers of the U.S. Congress. Foreign Relations subcommittees and House and Senate committees got the first crack at authorizing, then appropriating aid monies for specific countries. The United States had vital military interests in the Philippines. The Subic Bay Naval Base and Clark Air Base on Luzon Island were its largest facilities in the Pacific. They played an essential role as support hubs for its war in Vietnam, ensured the safe transport of oil supplies to its allies in Asia, and served to project its power in the region against the Soviet Union and China. Hence Marcos and his military establishment were essential to the considerable U.S. interests in the Philippines. In turn, Marcos's military had an ongoing need for hardware and training from the United States. This symbiotic relationship dictated the ebb and flow of military aid money each year.

By portraying U.S.-supplied security forces as the chief instrument keeping Marcos in power, the opposition hoped to either eliminate or reduce the amount of military aid earmarked for the Philippines. During deliberations on the 1973 aid bill, an amendment was introduced by Senator James Abourezk of South Dakota on December 5, 1973, that would deny assistance to any country that imprisoned its citizens for political purposes. An earlier Abourezk amendment to the Foreign Assistance Act of 1973 would have prohibited the use of aid funds for police, prisons, internal intelligence, or the maintenance of internal security forces. Both amendments were defeated, despite a campaign by MFP chapters to flood congressional committees with telegrams appealing for their enactment. The day before the debates, delegations of MFP members visited key committee members, among them Senators Daniel Inouye, Jacob Javits, Hubert H. Humphrey, and Edward Kennedy, and Representatives Bella Abzug and Lester Wolfe. The final version of the bill (a compromise between the House and Senate versions) approved $91.5 million in military aid for the Philippines.

The MFP had learned that its first lobbying venture needed more work. There was some comfort in the close margin of votes—44 to 41 in the Senate, 210 to 193 in the House. News reports said that many of the senators who voted against final approval of the bill claimed that too much money was being spent on foreign aid. Senator Frank Church, a senior member of the Committee on Foreign Relations, told the *New York Times* that "Americans are tired of seeing their tax dollars end up in the Swiss bank accounts of Cambodian generals or in the form of United States–built tanks used to kill Greek and Thai students."[1]

During the next round of shaping of the fiscal year 1974 aid package, a Senate Committee on Foreign Relations report made a pointed reference to the Philippines: "Today the problem is not the fall of friendly dominoes to communism, but their fall to military rule. Totalitarianism of the right should be as offensive to Washington as totalitarianism of the left. But the major recipients of our military aid—Korea, Thailand, the Philippines, Greece, and Taiwan—are hardly paragons of democratic government."[2] This time the military aid package to the Philippines was drastically cut—to $30,496,000; it was then reduced even further, to a requested $25,400,000 for 1975. The MFP was elated. They had urged every chapter to send letters and telegrams to all of the committee members.

It would soon become clear that the military aid issue demanded constant pressure on Congress and no lobbying letup. The aid package could shrink or expand from one year to the next. In 1976, for example, three members of the House—Edward Koch, Berkley Bedell, and Pete Stark—introduced amendments to reduce the Philippines' portion of the military aid package from $19.6 million to $6.6 million, a substantial cut. This was a follow-up to a previous amendment from Representative Tom Harkin that linked aid to human rights. The language was generic, and no mechanism was defined for its implementation. The Harkin amendment was introduced as a test case for the language, to make it apply to the Philippines. It failed to pass. Given the United States' utter dependence on its Philippine bases, it was unrealistic to think that Congress would risk losing them by cutting off all aid to Marcos. The best the exile lobbyists could hope for was a moderation in the regime's behavior, such as releasing political prisoners or dropping the use of torture.

The Philippine economy enjoyed robust growth during the early years of martial law, due in part to high prices for export commodities and increased tax revenues. But things soon began to deteriorate. World prices for the country's top exports—sugar and copper—began to fall. A $700 million trade deficit was being projected as a result. Payments, debt services, and interest charges on foreign loans reached $4.8 billion, up from $2.3 billion in 1973. Imported oil was costing $770 million a year. These sums depleted the dollar reserves from which the government paid for arms purchases. In an interview with *U.S. News & World Report*, Marcos complained: "We had to buy arms from Singapore, Taiwan and Europe because American help, agreed to and committed, either never arrived or arrived too late."[3] To his opponents, this meant that his dependence on U.S. arms was more crucial than ever.

At the same time, the lot of the ordinary Filipino deteriorated. "By the mid-1970s, seven out of every ten Filipinos were worse off economically as a result of martial law. Real wages for factory workers fell by about 30 percent in the first years of martial law, while consumer prices nearly tripled . . . The infant mortality rate was nearly twice as high in the Philippines as in South Korea." In addition, "A staggering 40 percent of all the nation's deaths were caused by malnutrition," partly because, "according to a confidential World Bank study in 1979, . . . 'one-third to one-half of the population is too poor to purchase and consume enough food.'"[4]

By the late 1980s, as the economy worsened and government revenues continued to decline, the regime's dependence on American foreign aid, both military and economic, grew. The aid package that the Reagan administration requested from Congress for fiscal year 1985 (October 1, 1984, to September 30, 1985—only three months before Marcos's downfall) totaled $230,959,000. The distribution of its components is illustrative of the areas where the United States was seeking to protect its interests. Specifically, the components covered the Economic Support Fund (ESF), Foreign Military Sales (FMS), and the Military Assistance Program (MAP). Together they totaled $184,000,000 out of the requested $230,959,000.

ESF, created in 1980 as part of the five-year (1980–84) bases agreement, was granted $200 million in funding during that period. For the new

1985–89 agreement, the administration requested a total of $475 million in ESF, to be given in five annual installments of $95 million. The funds were made available as grants from the U.S. Agency for International Development (USAID) to Imelda Marcos's Ministry of Human Settlements. A committee headed by Mrs. Marcos included representatives from the ministries of Defense, Agriculture, Industry, Public Works, Education, Budget, and Economic Planning. ESF funded projects for roads, schools, irrigation, markets, and housing. Between 1980 and 1984, $68 million in ESF funds, or 34 percent of the total, was spent on projects to improve the economic and social conditions of twenty-one cities and municipalities adjacent to the Clark and Subic bases Another $55 million was spent on the six provinces that surround those bases: Pampanga, Tarlac, Zambales, Bataan, Bulacan, and Nueva Ecija. In all, therefore, more than 61 percent of the money, $123 million out of $200 million, was disbursed to enhance the security of the U.S. bases by preventing the development of social unrest in the areas around them.

Funneling ESF funds through the Ministry of Human Settlements' widely diverse programs made them vulnerable to misuse. In one instance, an audit revealed that $1.1 million in interest was missing from the account. The *New York Times* reported that "government investigators suspect the missing money may have been channeled into the Marcos election campaign" against Corazon Aquino. It added that Marcos had ordered $1.75 million out of the special interest account "for payment of miscellaneous expenses . . . A total of $650,000 was returned to the fund after the election and the rest remains unaccounted for."[5] Three years later, the U.S. Attorney's Office in New York City charged that Marcos and his wife had illegally diverted $15 million in USAID grant funds to a personal bank account in Switzerland. The *Washington Post* reported that the $15 million was used to redeem Marcos's Philippine treasury notes for cash, which was wired in 1985 from the Federal Reserve Bank in New York to the Philippine Central Bank in Manila.[6]

ESF dollars were transferred to the Philippine treasury, and in exchange, the government made available an equivalent amount of pesos to finance the local costs of the ESF project. The government was then free to use the dollars for Philippine foreign exchange requirements, such as to help pay interest charges on the huge $25 billion foreign debt. In late 1983, more than $48 million remaining from the 1980–84 ESF funds was quickly released. Reported USAID during its February 6, 1984, presentation of its request to Congress: "It was concluded that accelerating ESF disbursements would help the Philippines in meeting conditions of an IMF program, . . . and would be instrumental in avoiding a financial disaster in the Philippines, while heading off spillover to other Asian nations."[7] The onerous interest payments on the foreign debt, and their effect on Philippine stability, were particularly worrisome for the Marcos administration. For 1985, the government wanted to use half of the $95 million in ESF funds for Philippine projects, and the other half as "non-project assistance," that is, "to address the Philippine balance of payments"—namely, the interest payments on loans from the IMF, the World Bank, the Asian Development Bank, and other multilateral development banks.

The Military Assistance Program funds, like ESF, were given as outright grants. During the five-year term of the previous bases agreement, the entire amount of $50 million had been disbursed during the first two years. For 1985, the Marcos government requested $25 million "in recognition of the serious economic situation" in the Philippines. MAP funds were used to buy defense equipment, mainly U.S.-made.

Foreign Military Sales credits were loans, not grants, for the purchase of American military equipment, which constituted most of the Philippine armed forces supply. The combined FMS/MAP request of $85 million for 1985 was a significant jump from the $50 million that had been requested in 1984. The total 1985–89 FMS/MAP request of $425 million reflected a 42 percent increase over the $250 million of the previous five years. FMS credit terms were severe. For 1985, the administration wanted half of the $60 million offered at 5 percent concessional rates (five years' grace/seven years' payback) because it recognized that "countries with low per capita incomes and severe debt-servicing problems may require some form of concessional financing."[8] The other half would carry market rates (ten years' grace/twenty years' payback).

How did the Philippines get itself into a $25 billion debt hole? Many knowledgeable observers have commented on the country's innate blessings, which boded well for developmental success. It possessed tremendous entrepreneurial talents, a well-educated workforce, and a vibrant community of economists and development specialists, and was receiving abundant overseas assistance. Yet economically, it had remained through the years "the sick man of Asia." Paul Hutchcroft, an American political scientist, laid the blame on "booty capitalism" and "rent capitalism." The former, also known as "crony capitalism," refers to "a powerful oligarchic business class that extracts privilege from a largely incoherent bureaucracy." Its practitioners during the Marcos era were less likely to foster new social classes to encourage change from within. "Rent capitalism" is a reference to "systems in which 'money is invested in arrangements for appropriating wealth which has already been produced rather than in [arrangements for actually] producing it.'"[9]

During the crumbling years of the Marcos regime, these forces shrank the economy by 9.5 percent in 1986; per capita income fell 15 percent to $822 from 1982; the peso's value against the dollar dropped to one-fourth of what it had been eight years earlier; unemployment stood at 15 percent, and underemployment at 40 percent; some $10 billion to $20 billion of investment capital had flowed overseas. In desperation, the regime had to borrow ever larger amounts of money to pay its bills until a full one-third of its export earnings were being used just to keep up with interest costs.

Other analysts saw the hand of the creditors in churning the economic mess. In a landmark work "based on 6,000 pages of secret documents," Walden Bello details the alleged role of the World Bank in impoverishing the Philippines. Between 1971 and 1982, the Bank had funded $3.38 billion worth of development aid to the country. But much of that money, according to Bello and his co-authors, was channeled to the Bank's two key objectives: rural and urban "pacification" development programs to defuse unrest. A drastic liberalization or restructuring of Philippine industry would have opened up the country more completely to the flow of U.S. capital and commodities. Both objectives had failed, they claimed. Pacification fell apart because the Bank refused "to grant 'beneficiaries' any meaningful role in making decisions on issues that affected their lives." Export-oriented industrialization collapsed because at that time it was making the country more dependent on a world market that was being savaged by an international recession.[10]

Bello, who received his Ph.D. in 1975 from Cornell University in New York, joined the KDP in 1973 and devoted his efforts to lobbying and research. When he tried to renew his passport in 1974, he said in a 2002 interview,

> it was confiscated without explanation. So I was effectively stateless for the next several years. The KDP was now the central focus of my life. I taught at the City College in San Francisco, the State University of New York, and at [the University of California in] Berkeley for about four years—not in order to pursue an academic career, but to survive . . . It was when we were researching the question of US bilateral aid to Marcos that we realized how much of it was being channelled through

the World Bank. The role of multilateral institutions—and the Bank in particular—in the Philippines dwarfed direct American support. That's where my own interest began. I had no formal background in economics; it was all on-the-job training. Figuring out the contours of this comprehensive development strategy became a passionate, all-consuming task that eventually led to [the] book.[11]

Indeed, the book represented not only the collaborative efforts of several authors but also the result of clandestine snooping worthy of real-life spies. As Bello described it in a 2008 speech:

The problem was that the lack of transparency of the Bank meant that we couldn't get any information about the Bank programs. The only information that we got were sanitized press releases. It became clear that to show what the Bank was doing and expose it, the only way was to get the documents from within the Bank itself. At first, we slowly formed a network of informants within the Bank. These were acquaintances, liberals with a conscience. Our work was part of a process of building what was effectively a counter-intelligence network not only within the Bank but also within the State Department and other agencies of the US government.

Well, these people started to occasionally bring us some documents, but this was a tedious—although necessary—process. The information was not enough, so we thought that it was necessary to resort to more radical means. So, my associates and I investigated the patterns of behavior of Bank people and we realized that there were some times in the year when there was nobody in the Bank: Thanksgiving, Christmas, New Year, July 4, Memorial Day, etc. On those days and over a period of three years, we went to the Bank pretending that we were returning from a mission, with our ties askew, and that we were just coming from Africa, India, etc. The security guards always asked for our ID's and when we pretended to fumble for them and as we looked so tired, they said 'OK, just go inside.' It always worked. As you can imagine, security was quite lax on those days.

Once we were inside, we were like kids let loose in a candy store. We took as many documents as we could, and not only on the Philippines, and photocop[ied] them using the Bank facilities. This happened over three years.

The documents—some 3000 pages of them on practically every Bank-supported project and program in the country provided an unparalleled look at the workings of a close relationship between two non-transparent authoritarian institutions, the World Bank and the Marcos regime. First, we held press conferences to expose the documents piece by piece, to the embarrassment of both the Bank and the Marcos regime . . .

But we were quite careful going about it and we were not able to tell the real story about how we got the documents until after 10 years (1992), when . . . the statute of limitations for criminal prosecution in the US had lapsed. My associates and I could have gotten 25 years in jail had we been caught breaking into the Bank.[12]

A high-water mark in the 1975 lobbying campaign was the hearings called by Representative Donald M. Fraser of Minnesota, chairman of the House Subcommittee on International Organizations and Movements. The topic was "Human Rights in South Korea and the Philippines: Implications for U.S. Foreign Policy." The exiles had finally gained their most coveted appearance in the halls of Congress. For three full days, on June 3, 5, and 17, people spoke out against the regime, including MFP officers Manglapus and Alvarez; Fr. Bruno Hicks, a Franciscan who served in Negros province, central Philippines; Fr. Joseph O'Hare, who taught for a number of years at a Jesuit university in Manila; Gerald Hill and Edward Morris, American lawyers who visited the Philippines; the Rev. Paul Wilson, a Disciples of Christ missionary who had been imprisoned for sixteen days by the military; and Primitivo Mijares, former chairman of the Media Advisory Council. The lone defender of the regime was the former Philippine ambassador Amelito Mutuc, who admitted that the government was still holding some six thousand detainees.

At the hearings, Philip C. Habib, assistant secretary for East Asia and Pacific affairs, went further than any other senior official in criticizing the Philippine government. He said that while Manila had made some improvements in social, economic, and administrative areas, "we do not believe that the ends justify or require the curtailment of human rights."[13] Manglapus described the difficulties of congressional lobbying. "We were not very well organized, not till about 1975. Marcos portrayed himself as a staunch and heroic friend of the U.S. We had our high points, when we were able to get the ear of the State Department. And later on, key members of the Senate spoke for us—Kennedy, Cranston—and in the House, Solarz, Leach, Tom Harkin, Tony Hall."[14] In the early 1970s, Manglapus recalled that he had to plead for appointments when he wanted to see members of Congress. "We now have much better access. Five years ago we could not get to first base with most Republicans. But now we are much more warmly received."[15]

Meanwhile, reports from contacts in the Philippine opposition warned of widespread torture of political prisoners. At the same time, the U.S. media were increasingly publishing accounts of torture by military regimes in Chile, Greece, and South Korea. It was an opportunity for the exiles to spotlight the human rights situation in the Philippines under Marcos. Letters from former detainees were collected. These as well as copies of a survey compiled by the Task Force Detainees of the Association of Major Religious Superiors in the Philippines were packaged into kits for the MFP chapters to use. Plans were laid out to expose the practice by the Philippine security forces at the annual September opening of the United Nations General Assembly in New York. The timing was auspicious: the UN was also marking the twenty-fifth anniversary of the Universal Declaration of Human Rights. Amnesty International, the London-based group that sought freedom for political prisoners, issued a 224-page report containing evidence of torture in sixty-four countries over the previous ten years. Seven of those countries were in Asia, and the Philippines was among them. The exiles' allies in the religious community responded strongly. On November 14, 1974, the United Church Board for World Ministries sent a letter of concern to President Gerald Ford. In the United States and Canada, the National Council of Churches, the Provincial Superiors of the Society of the Divine Word Missionaries, the United Church of Christ, and the United Presbyterian Church shot off letters to Manila.

Marcos freed 1,076 detainees in December, although he had claimed two months earlier, during a television interview, that the government had "just released the last of the detention prisoners."[16] A news report said that "the Philippine military, responding to charges of torture made by religious groups, took action yesterday against seven enlisted men and five officers."[17] At the time, the military had never admitted to or charged any security personnel with using torture.

The Fraser hearings, already a major morale boost to the exiles, would have faded away after the first flurry of publicity if not for a series of bizarre incidents involving one of the witnesses, which kept the hearings fresh for weeks. Primitivo Mijares, a Filipino newspaperman, was the administration's chief press censor and propagandist. In late 1974 he arrived in San Francisco, and at a press conference on February 20, 1975, he announced that he was defecting. His declared motive was that he could no longer accept Marcos's corrupt rule, which he knew at first hand. The defection of a high-level official with an intimate knowledge of martial law affairs was bad enough. But to tell all at a congressional hearing was worse. On the witness stand, Mijares submitted a twenty-four-page memo about "vote fraud, corporate theft, payoffs, illegal jailings and general corruption."[18]

Two hours before Mijares took the stand, he claimed that Marcos aides had offered him a $50,000 bribe to dissuade him from testifying. They had deposited the check in the San Francisco branch of Lloyds Bank of California in his name and that of Ambassador Trinidad Alconcel. Undeterred, Mijares went ahead with his testimony and informed Fraser about the bribe attempt. Alconcel then withdrew the money. For a foreign government to bribe a congressional witness was a flagrant criminal offense, and Fraser notified the U.S. Justice Department to investigate. The Philippine foreign undersecretary, Jose Ingles, confirmed the existence of the $50,000 check but alleged that it was intended for use in starting a pro-government newspaper in San Francisco. The money was also to be used, he claimed, to gather information on U.S.-based groups that were plotting to kill Marcos and Imelda. Mijares later stated that another $100,000 was offered to stop publication of a book he was writing, subsequently published as *The Conjugal Dictatorship of Ferdinand and Imelda Marcos I*.

On January 6, 1977, Mijares disappeared. He was reportedly last seen at the San Francisco International Airport in the company of a Philippine official. Rumors swirled that somehow he was lured back to Manila. His fifteen-year-old son was also missing, and on June 18, Reuters reported that the boy's body had been identified at an undertaker's facility in suburban Manila. He had been beaten and stabbed to death.[19]

CHAPTER 8

Down with Rhetoric!

Turning to Radical Means

At the seventh MFP convention in San Mateo, California, on September 5, 1979, the members took stock of their work. The year before, some encouraging milestones had been achieved—a highly talented escapee had joined the movement; there had been an appearance and testimony before a House committee; contacts had been established with Muslim opponents of the government in the southern island of Mindanao.

A new American president, Jimmy Carter, had taken office in 1977. At a press conference on November 16, 1977, he declared, "I think the allocation of foreign aid and the normal friendship of our country would be determined or affected certainly by the attitude of those countries toward human rights." (Carter would later shelve any interest in Philippine human rights after a renewal of the bases agreement was negotiated.) Human rights advocates had retained their seats in the new Congress, including two in the Senate—James Abourezk and George McGovern—who introduced human rights provisions into any military aid appropriations. But across the oceans, dark clouds hovered. In 1978 the KBL party had won control of the new legislature, and Imelda Marcos had been appointed to the cabinet. At the end of 1979, Marcos would call for nationwide elections for governors and mayors. His KBL candidates were expected to sweep the field (which they ultimately did).

And so, as some two hundred MFP members assembled at the Villa Hotel in San Mateo, a suburb of San Francisco, to map out their next moves, they were in a combative mood. Was there no stopping the man? Where was the light at the end of this long, dark tunnel, which was already six years in the making? They had received reports that the moderate op-position in the Philippines was likewise frustrated and angry, and even—surprisingly—calling for violence. These were not the radical leftists who had always endorsed aggressive means and followed their convictions by joining the militant National Democratic Front (NDF) and its military arm, the New People's Army (NPA), in the hills. The moderate voices who were now advocating for a shift in tactics reasoned that peaceful means had gotten them nowhere, and that the dictatorship was as entrenched as ever. It was time to take up arms. But they would do it their way, without the NDF or the NPA, whose anti-democratic ideology they abhorred.

Thus was born an urban guerrilla group who called themselves the Light-A-Fire movement (LAF). Their weapon of choice was homemade bombs. Beginning in August 1979, bombs exploded in several buildings in Manila. The targets were symbolic—banks, Rustan's shopping mall, a casino, the Plaza Hotel—all known to be owned by Marcos cronies. The Commission on Elections Building was a prime target because of the com-mission's role in manipulating the legislative elections. Among the LAF's leaders were two Harvard-trained businessmen: Gaston Ortigas, associ-ate dean for faculty and programs at the Manila-based Asian Institute of Management (AIM); and Eduardo Olaguer, a professor at AIM and chief executive of a transportation company. The bombs they devised consisted of gift-wrapped cardboard boxes, in which a hidden magnetic system trig-gered a mousetrap that ignited the bomb with a match.[1] The LAF's objec-tive, according to pamphlets distributed by Olaguer, was "to light a fire against Marcos, both literally through arson, and figuratively by sparking a revolt."[2] He was inspired by the turnout on the streets of Manila, where masses of residents had banged pots and pans and honked their car horns in protesting the conduct of the April 6 elections, which Aquino lost.

"Our members are telling us that we are all talk, talk, talk," an MFP member reported at the meeting. Someone made a motion that they should drop from their charter the mandate to employ only "nonviolent means" to achieve their goals. The resolution passed. It would subsequently be re-membered as the "Armalite Resolution" because when pledges were sought at the meeting to fund these nonpeaceful methods, the minimum U.S. cash donation requested was "one unit of material support." That happened to match the price of a U.S.-made Armalite infantry rifle.[3] The resolution was viewed as a historic turnaround by the other exile oppositionists. From the outset, the MFP had built their base and its appeal by propagating a nonviolent position. Now they were advocating a turn to force.

In an eight-page manifesto titled "The Christian Force," Manglapus reasoned that "we Filipinos have reached the last boundaries of our patience. We have despaired of futile appeals. Now we must act. How shall we act? The Catholic Bishops of the Philippines are opposed to mindless violence, but they have just reminded us that Pope Paul VI justified the use of force against 'manifest, long-standing tyranny which would do great damage to fundamental rights and dangerous harm to the common good of the economy.' Such is the tyranny of Ferdinand Marcos."[4] Bonifacio Gillego, an MFP officer with avowed leftist tendencies, said that "when we began to talk guerrillas and armed struggle, that was where Raul disagreed. He wanted to use [force] as a spark or a spur that would lead to mass movement. It was a bit unrealistic but it was his thinking at that time."[5]

When asked about the LAF and the April 6 Liberation Movement (A6LM) bombings, Manglapus replied, "MFP was never officially linked to both. However, MFP members had personal, not organizational, contacts with them. There was no official endorsement of both."[6] Alvarez confirmed that "we worked with the Light-A-Fire people together with Olaguer and Gillego. But Raul did not know this. We felt that he was too statesmanlike. So we organized this side force" within the MFP without Manglapus's approval.[7] LAF and A6LM activities and their links to the MFP "were kept on a need-to-know basis," said Steve Psinakis, an MFP officer. "Very few knew. Manglapus was not a party, was not informed of the inner details, while Ninoy was in the thick of things."[8] Psinakis, who hosted the San Francisco gathering, was identified in a newspaper story as the personal connection that Manglapus alluded to.[9] A colleague, Ben Lim, was caught on December 12 at the Manila International Airport bringing in explosives from the United States, including blasting caps and incendiary materials. He confessed that Psinakis had supplied them. In Olaguer's Manila safe house, where he was captured, the government recovered a list of the bombing targets—the newspaper offices of the *Times Journal* and the *Daily Express* and the Kanlaon Broadcasting System, all propaganda arms of the regime—as well as the office of the Herdis Company, a business conglomerate owned by a cousin of Imelda.

Ortigas eluded capture, following the escape route pioneered by earlier exiles through the southern back door. Through the network of church and diplomatic contacts that Manglapus had established for the escape of his family as well as those of Gillego and Planas, he managed to reach the Malaysian capital of Kuala Lumpur. For months he holed up inside the South East Asian Hotel until the proper asylum papers were processed.

After gaining admittance to the United States in May 1980, he promptly joined the MFP. He had previous links with Manglapus: in 1970, in connection with the campaign by the latter's Christian Social Movement to elect delegates to the Constitutional Convention, and again in 1974, during a visit to Boston to complete his Harvard University dissertation, when the two men had a discussion about Ortigas's impressions of the movement. He said that he found it very disorganized, a not altogether novel description, since the MFP was still amorphous only two years into its formation.

Eventually, because of his excellent management skills, Ortigas was named the organization's executive director. He was no ivory tower technocrat, having held previous jobs that required him to interact frequently with people at all levels. He had been a factory supervisor with the U.S.-owned Procter and Gamble manufacturing plant (where he "agitate[d] his fellow managers to fight for equal treatment with their American expatriate counterparts"); he had founded the first personnel consulting firm in the country; he had managed a worker-owned textile firm; and he had taught a production management course at Ateneo de Manila's Graduate School of Business Administration.[10] He applied all of these experiences in untangling the affairs of the MFP. "[The] first element was commitment, making elections and ongoing political activity conditions for MFP national council membership. This would sideline dilettantes, careerists, and weaklings from key positions. The second was decentralization. Concentration of leadership in very few people had become very dangerous," wrote Sylvia Mayuga in a biography of Ortigas.[11]

Fluellen Ortigas, Gaston's cousin and also another exile-escapee, said that he "was trying to streamline and systematize MFP, which is not easy to do with a volunteer organization."[12] At the same time, he felt the pain of having to place his career indefinitely on hold and communicate secretly with his distant family while devoting his full efforts to the movement. He was also troubled by the virtual eradication of their Light-A-Fire movement. For the first seven months after the initial suspects were rounded up, no bombs exploded. The government crowed that the wild, misguided dreams to destabilize the regime had failed miserably. Aquino, however, warned that the lull would not last. It was a few months later, in May 1980, that he came to the United States for heart surgery, and in his first speech after being released from the hospital, he spoke about a new class of angry citizens, people who had the talent, the financial resources, and the connections to unleash a new round of violence. They would be known as the April 6 Liberation Movement (A6LM).

Another project that the attendees at the MFP conference in San Francisco resolved to advance was the "Nur Misuari connection." Nur Misuari was the head of the Moro National Liberation Movement (MNLF), which has been conducting a Muslim armed insurgency since 1968 in several provinces on the southern island of Mindanao, seeking a broad measure of self-rule. The roots of the insurgency dated back to the 1950s, when Christian migrants from other parts of the country began to settle in areas occupied by the native Muslim residents, popularly known as the Moros. They resented the loss of land and economic opportunities. Indeed, the Moros, proud of their heritage and with a long history of resisting outsiders as far back as the Spanish colonial era, rebelled against any attempt by Manila-based administrations to impose their authority. During the 1960s, feuds between the Christians and the Moros had escalated into violence, which spread in scope and size. (By the late 2000s, an estimated 80,000 to 200,000 army, insurgent, and civilian lives had been claimed by the hostilities.) Misuari refused to have his forces lay down their weapons, largely supplied by Muslim Libya, as Marcos ordered when he declared martial law.

The MFP saw an opportunity to "open a dialogue for possible areas of cooperation" with Misuari against the regime.[13] Gillego, who conceived the idea, argued that Misuari might agree to provide arms, training facilities, and a refuge for asylees. The Sulu archipelago, stretching from Mindanao toward the waters of Malaysia, had been the gateway for MFP escapees. "The Muslims are our Filipino brothers. And if they have the wherewithal to help us, we must welcome their assistance," he said. Serge Osmena III added, "I also feel that Marcos will be affected by a report that the MFP has 'established' links with the Muslims. Psycho-war?"[14]

Three MFP emissaries—Osmena, former congressman Raul Daza, and Cesar Climaco Jr., the former mayor of Zamboanga City—arrived in Dakar, Senegal, on April 25, 1978, to establish initial contacts with some Misuari aides. Manglapus followed up with a visit to Tripoli, Libya, in May. News of the meetings, which the MFP had kept secret, leaked to the Manila newspapers. In a frantic note to Manglapus, a Manila contact said that he was offering Misuari a merger to provide "unlimited financial assistance; secession of Mindanao from the Philippines; flying Muslim flag alone in Mindanao." He urgently advised Manglapus "to decry such false reporting." Manila's press had insinuated that the MFP was encouraging secession. In an open letter to Marcos, Manglapus responded that the MNLF "have assured us they do not seek secession. The prompt restoration of our democracy will bring them true autonomy and end the bloody conflict in our South."[15]

Misuari did agree to help escapees. "But as it happened, after 1978 there were hardly any more," said Manglapus.[16] Gillego, perhaps more than anybody else among the escapees, understood the need for a safe haven. The day after martial law was announced in 1972, "there was an eerie silence," he remembered, "no TV, no radio, no newspapers. The telephone rang. Ernie said: *Sibat na*! (Run!) Martial law has been declared!" "Why? What did I do wrong?" he asked.[17] Ernie Rondon, a fellow elected delegate to the Constitutional Convention, was working to draft a new constitution to replace the 1935 charter. He and several of the other delegates tried to block proposals to extend Marcos's term in the new constitution.

A second call came twenty minutes later from Mila Albert, the wife of Captain Carlos Albert, Gillego's former boss in an army intelligence unit. She advised Gillego to flee. Again he said that he wouldn't. About eight A.M., a nephew arrived in a van at his house in the Manila suburb of Quezon City, with firm instructions from Gillego's sister to take him to San Francisco del Monte, a Manila neighborhood, where he could hide in a friend's house. Thirty minutes after he left in his slippers, he said that two jeeps and an army truck arrived and surrounded his house. There, sleeping on the living room couches, they found three overnight guests from his home province of Sorsogon in the central Philippines. One was the mayor of San Magdalena, who had come seeking contributions for a town fiesta; the others were a police officer and his son, needing Gillego's help for the early release of his retirement pay benefits.

Thus began Gillego's life as a fugitive. For six years he moved around within Sorsogon and Samar provinces. He carried with him a residence certificate that identified him as Andres Delgado ("Andres" after a revolutionary hero against Spain named Andres Bonifacio, and "Delgado" because he was, after all, a constitutional delegate). The alias was chosen with care, he said, so that if he was suddenly addressed by that name, he could respond instantly. "My military intelligence training," he remarked.[18] Indeed, he had valid reasons to assume an alias. Many years later, after Marcos was deposed and Gillego was back in the Philippines, he obtained the intelligence file that the army had used to track his movements. In it was a presidential order listing him (the third among twenty names) as someone who was to be arrested and detained, based on "verified reports" that he had "engaged in subversion and other acts inimical to public order and national security."[19] Gillego, his file said, was a "national target" operating in the Bicol region, an area composed of several central provinces, including Sorsogon. The file included ten pages of detailed reports—every speech he had delivered as a delegate, every paper he had presented at a conference, every article he had published, and information on the activists he had met, every appearance he had made as a speaker at rallies against Marcos, and all of his meetings with student groups. From the reports, the government had concluded that Gillego was an avowed Communist. And when he later joined the MFP, it gave them reason to charge the group as harboring an anti-government activist. One item in the dossier read:

> His true color was finally betrayed in 1973 when he became identified with the KM [Kabataang Makabayan—a youth leftist group] Legaspi City chapter. In the same year, there was a report that he, with an undetermined number of followers, joined the insurgent ranks . . . that he directed NPA [New People's Army] operations in Sorsogon. The Moon Theater, the hideout of the subject in Bulan, Sorsogon, was utilized as a temporary NPA hideout and conference room of the top NPA leaders. His intelligence background in the Armed Forces of the Philippines must have qualified him to be counted among the NPA brasses.[20]

In the United States, Gillego drew on his intimate knowledge of the Philippine military establishment. Testifying as an MFP officer before the U.S. Foreign Operations Subcommittee of the House Committee on Appropriations (which sets the amounts of foreign aid) on April 11, 1984, he described the militarization trends of martial law. One example he gave was a National Security Code decree that allowed the posting of security agents "in all national and government offices, agencies and instrumentalities."[21] On U.S. foreign aid, he recommended during the hearing that a certification process be implemented as a condition for the release of aid funds. The certification (similar to Congress's attempt to withhold aid to El Salvador until a series of reforms had been implemented and the death squads had been reined in) would require the White House to submit regular reports on whether and how and to what effect the Philippine military had minimized torture and illegal detentions. Those reports would be the basis for determining whether Congress should continue providing aid that had already been appropriated.

Gillego enlisted in the Philippine army in 1955 and served as a platoon leader in Korea, after which he attended a course in military attaché training at the Johns Hopkins School of Advanced International Studies in Washington, D.C. Such training included intelligence gathering. The study tour, he remarked ironically in 1995, was his reward for his role in capturing the leaders of an anti-government group in the 1950s known as the Hukbalahap or Huks. Its leaders were accused of being Communists.[22] From 1957 to 1960, he applied his training as the military attaché with the Philippine embassy in Burma (now Myanmar). His dossier noted that there was "no significant report about the subject between 1978 and 1979." This was true because during this period he had managed to escape from the country. While he was on the run, the only people he contacted for help were people he knew well. He was rebuffed time and again, and at one time he broke down in tears when a school administrator whom he considered a close friend would not or could not offer support. On January 12, 1978, he smuggled a note to then Congressman Ralph Recto, saying in part: "By the time you receive this I may be on the way south to establish the connections for my exit to the initial destination. Please identify me to your friends in Sabah and Kuala Lumpur because I have no papers whatsoever . . . Barring delays and incidents, expect to hear from me anytime in February or March. God be with us in this venture."[23]

Divine help he sorely needed. "I did not know anybody. Nobody told me about the route. I was going blind. Raul told me to find a way to get to Sabah." He flew to Leyte, a province in the central Philippines, then to Cebu, to Zamboanga City, and to Bongao, the capital of Sulu. Across the sea, Sabah beckoned, a galaxy away. "In Tawi-tawi, I got to the beach and hung around in a bar. The cashier looked familiar. After some small talk he said he was from my hometown Bulan, Sorsogon, a retired Philippine Constabulary trooper. Then I told him the truth, that I was looking for a way out."[24] A motorized canoe dropped him on Sabah, where he stayed three nights. He called Fr. John Lee, a Manglapus contact. Messages flew back and forth between the United Nations human rights commissioner, the Christian Democratic World Union in Geneva (allied with Manglapus's Christian Social Movement), and the U.S. embassy in Kuala Lumpur, which issued him a parole asylum pass. There, dressed in a T-shirt, he boarded a Singapore Airlines plane to Washington, D.C., where Manglapus and his son-in-law Ben Maynigo were on hand to meet him in April 1978.

Gillego brought with him two traits that served the movement well—an incisive, analytical mind and a voracious appetite for information. With his army intelligence background, he set himself a task close to his heart: documenting the politicization of the military establishment by Marcos and its dependence on U.S. aid. He compiled two studies that circulated among the exile groups: "The Spy Network of Marcos in the U.S." and "Grammar of U.S. Assistance to the Marcos Dictatorship."

In 1982 he embarked on a project that would consume him for the next several months. He was determined to debunk Marcos's record as a war hero. In government-issued propaganda, Marcos had always been portrayed as a fearless guerrilla fighter whose exploits against the Japanese occupying forces helped America to liberate Filipinos. He held up this record as a defining aspect of his character as a leader. During his state visit to Washington in September 1982, "Defense Secretary Caspar Weinberger presented him with a case displaying U.S. medals supposedly awarded to him in World War II. They included the Distinguished Service Cross, the Silver Star and the Purple Heart. President Reagan complimented him at a special ceremony for fighting 'valiantly' on the U.S. side against Japan."[25] At the same event, the Philippine embassy distributed a brochure, "Friends In War: Ferdinand Marcos E. Marcos in the Pacific War, 1941–45." It listed thirty-two American and Philippine medals that he supposedly had been awarded during that period.

Gillego knew exactly where to check the veracity of the medals, particularly the American awards. At 9700 Page Avenue in the St. Louis suburb of Overland, Missouri, is the National Personnel Records Center. It holds some 80 million records of military personnel, dating as far back as the Philippine-American War of 1899–1903. There Gillego and Dr. Arturo Taca, who happened to be the president of the St. Louis MFP chapter, began the laborious research. The result of their efforts, "The Marcos Medals: A Study in Extrapolation," was published on December 4, 1981, in the Philippine English weekly *We Forum*, a Manila-based publication critical of the Marcos administration. Gillego's study documented instances of double counting, medals that were not medals at all but rather campaign citations given to all war participants, and one medal given on his birthday in 1972, long after the war was over. An enraged Marcos ordered the publication closed on December 17, 1982, and had all fifteen staffers arrested. A 40 million peso libel suit was also filed.

Congressman Lane Evans, a member of the U.S. House Committee on Veterans Affairs, had the exposé published in the *Congressional Record*, with a cautionary note to his colleagues that as the United States began in 1984 to renegotiate its bases agreement, "we should re-examine just who and what is this man with whom we are dealing."[26] That should have ended the furor. But the *Washington Post* decided to check the validity of the three Silver Star medals awarded to Marcos by the Pentagon. Reporter

John Sharkey examined official military histories, personal memoirs, and portions of Marcos's personal files at the National Personnel Records Center, and conducted interviews with Philippine and American survivors of the war. His research cast doubt on whether the medals were actually awarded. "The issue of the medals," he wrote, "is more than a matter of passing historical interest. Marcos' political opponents say that his record as a well-decorated war hero fighting shoulder-to-shoulder with the United States has given him an image in this country that encourages Americans to overlook his authoritarian style of government and abuses of human rights."[27]

In the course of researching the medals, Gillego alerted Taca that there was also something suspicious about a guerrilla unit, Ang Mga Maharlika (the Noble Ones), that Marcos had headed during the war. Attempts starting in August 1982 to gain access to the Maharlika archives at the Records Center got Taca nowhere. He received one bureaucratic excuse after another to delay his access to the records. In April 1983 he was told that they were being "reclassified" and could not be seen at that time. Yet when he followed up in September 1984, he was told by two archivists that Philippine army personnel had been going through the Philippine archives, apparently to prevent another questionable medal exposé. Before the records were transferred to the National Archives in Washington, D.C., Taca was able to examine some references to Maharlika.

American historian Alfred W. McCoy, then a professor of history at the University of New South Wales in Sydney, Australia, discovered the transferred Maharlika documents while researching a book on World War II in the Philippines during the summer of 1985. He took them to the *New York Times* in January 1986. Jeff Gerth, an investigative reporter for the *Times*, knew Gillego and gave him a call. "Have you heard about Maharlika?" he asked. "Yes," Gillego responded. The *Times* ran its story on the front page, scooping the *Washington Post* by a day because of the McCoy trove of records.[28] While the *Times* described at length the lack of documentation to prove Maharlika's existence, the *Post* revealed in equally exhaustive detail that Marcos "actually worked on behalf of Philippine politicians who collaborated with the Japanese occupation of the islands." The principal politician named in the article is Jose P. Laurel, who served as president of the Philippines during the Japanese occupation from October 1943 until the end of the war. It was Laurel, then a Supreme Court justice, who overturned Marcos's conviction in 1938 for killing his father's political rival in a 1935 congressional election.

The army archives listed ninety guerrilla units with a total manpower of 162,000, ranging in strength from 5 men to 35,000 men. After the war, Filipino guerrillas asked the U.S. Army to recognize their service with the units so that they could receive back pay and benefits. Marcos submitted such a request for his Maharlika unit, which he claimed he had led from 1942 to 1944, giving the number of members as 300 men at one point and as 8,200 men another time. In rejecting his request, U.S. Army records cited the following reasons, among others, as listed by the *New York Times*:

- Maharlika had not actually been in the field fighting the Japanese and had not "contributed materially to the eventual defeat of the enemy";
- Maharlika had no "definite organization," and "adequate records were not maintained";
- Maharlika was not controlled adequately "because of the desertion of its commanding officer," Mr. Marcos, who eventually joined an American military unit while in northern Luzon at the time of the American invasion;
- Maharlika could not possibly have operated over the wide area it claimed because of problems of terrain, communications, and Japanese "antiresistance activities";
- Many members apparently lived at home, supporting their families by means of farming or other civilian pursuits, and assisted the guerrilla units on a part-time basis only.[29]

An army researcher at the Records Center concluded that Marcos's claims about Maharlika were "fraudulent," "preposterous," and "a malicious criminal act." The *Times* noted that throughout his reelection campaign speeches, Marcos had "referred to his war record and guerrilla experiences in part to show that he is better able than his opponent, Corazon C. Aquino, to handle the present Communist insurgency."[30] Both were campaigning for the presidential election scheduled on February 7, 1986.

Manglapus, who had put Gillego on the medals story, emphasized the value of personal attacks on Marcos: "When you expose him as a fraud, when you reduce his credibility all over the world, you make it impossible for him to govern. To me, it's worth exchanging five newspapers more if you are able to destroy the credibility of the dictator. Because Marcos is sensitive to that. Marcos understands that although you attack everything else in his government, as long as you don't attack him, he will stay in power. You've got to attack him. You've got to be personal, you see. That's the problem. If you do not become personal, then you're not going to solve the problem at all. He will allow you to destroy his [prime minister] Virata. He will allow you to destroy even Imelda. But he will never allow you to destroy him."[31]

For Gillego, a career army man, the faked medals and Maharlika exposés were intended to do more than merely deflate the reputation of a "strongman" leader. Marcos was commander-in-chief of the armed forces, and his shady credentials would dishearten his troops. Indeed, by 1985, "tensions and morale problems" were already plaguing the estimated 150,000-member armed forces.[32] A group of younger officers organized a band they called the Reform Armed Forces Movement (RAM) to show their displeasure over how General Fabian Ver, a staunch Marcos loyalist and head of the intelligence services, had built up his power over other, more senior officers.

On November 21, 1985, Colonel Alexander Bacalla, the assistant deputy chief of staff for civil-military operations at General Headquarters, publicly defected in Washington and joined the MFP. Two other officers defected to the movement—Lt. Col. Jaime Gopilan of the army and Major Vicente Carag of the air force. They were presented at a press conference in Los Angeles, California. This was an alarming trend that troubled the regime. It quickly suspended any trips by armed forces officers to the United States.

CHAPTER 9

The War of Words

Winning Hearts and Minds

To sustain momentum, the MFP scheduled annual conventions beginning in 1974. For symbolic purposes, they were held in September to mark the anniversaries of the declaration of martial law and the founding of the organization. At these conventions, the members refined their lobbying and organizing techniques and mapped out new projects. For instance, the 1974 Chicago convention launched the anti-torture campaign and a project to set up an offshore radio transmitter.

Yearly conventions also kept the other groups alive. At the KDP's fifth annual conference in 1978, one hundred activists gathered at the Georgetown University Law Center in Washington, D.C. At the ninth annual conference of the FFP at Peekskill, New York, in 1983, fifty participants huddled for three days of workshops. They reported adding five thousand names to petitions against the U.S. bases, sponsoring forums in twenty states, campaigning against the extradition treaty, and buying a $1,500 ad in the *Washington Post* to protest the 1982 state visit of Marcos. The speakers at and organizers of these conferences were often the same activists who led the two organizations.

Radio Free Philippines was conceived to broadcast from international waters off the Philippines. A site was considered near Sabah, on the string of islands leading from the southern island of Mindanao. There were consultations with lawyers. A detailed business plan, with cost estimates and personnel, was put together. The equipment was bought, but before it could be set up, the local Mindanao supporter of the project was removed from office. His identity and the proposed location of the transmitter could not be disclosed until the station went on the air. Stored at a rental space in California, the equipment disappeared when the storage company went bankrupt. That ended the venture.

The U.S. opposition groups ranged all over the country, looking for any local opportunity to mount a public protest. In 1981 they forced Tufts University's well-regarded Fletcher School of Law and Diplomacy to cancel a $1.5 million grant from Imelda Marcos to honor her husband.[1] The grant would have established a Marcos Chair of East Asian and Pacific Studies at the Massachusetts school. Eighty faculty members signed a letter of protest. Reasons for rejecting the money included critical editorials in the Tufts student newspaper as well as negative reaction in U.S. newspapers. When Mrs. Marcos visited the school in 1977 to announce the grant, more than one thousand protesters disrupted her visit.

But there was nothing like an appearance on American soil by Marcos himself to cause a major ruckus. The 94th Annual Convention of the American Newspaper Publishers Association (ANPA) in Honolulu on April 23, 1980, presented such a rare occasion: a gathering of about two thousand influential opinion makers, representing all the major news publications in the U.S. It was Marcos's first visit to the U.S. in fourteen years.

Marcos received widespread publicity when he addressed the convention. In response, the MFP told the ANPA that as American journalists dedicated to the truth, it was only fair that they should allow another point of view. And so the ANPA arranged the next day for Manglapus and other MFP speakers to speak, even though they were not part of the formal program. Manglapus reminded the journalists that Marcos had shut down or taken over twenty-two English-language, four vernacular, two Spanish-language, and sixty community newspapers. Among the six thousand political detainees, he told them, were publishers and journalists like them.

The exiles attempted to set up a shortwave radio transmitter for their speeches, well aware that the bigger, more important audience for their messages resided in their homeland, not in the United States. Filipino visitors to the U.S., exposed to U.S. media reports about the Philippines, complained in their letters home that it was difficult to get a true sense of the Philippine political picture because the local press was forbidden to publish negative news and commentary. The exiles urged Filipinos in the United States to enclose U.S. press clippings in their letters home. These were then copied and circulated there, in a practice described as "Xerox journalism."

Reflecting their bias for a free press and scorn for the controlled press in the Philippines, the major U.S. media consistently gave the exiles favorable coverage. By and large, the exiles had won the media war in the United States against the regime. "The Philippine Government has suffered from a negative image in the United States principally because critical reports by the 'liberal' press, and constant propaganda of oppositionists, have not been countered effectively," wrote Raul Ch. Rabe, consul general of the Philippine consulate in Honolulu, Hawaii, in a letter to the minister of foreign affairs in Manila. "The barrage of negative reports has been overwhelming... Our personnel abroad are also working from an innate disadvantage—as employees of the Philippine Government, their statements are naturally taken as self-serving and lacking in credibility. In turn, because of this realization, many of our personnel have not been too eager to appear in mass media, particularly in debates with the opposition."[2]

The generally critical attitude of the U.S. media acutely troubled Mrs. Marcos. She summoned the American ambassador, Michael Armacost, to express her husband's "anxieties about his upcoming [1982] visit to the USA," Armacost wrote in his report. "As a shrewd politician he is undoubtedly trying to sort out the political benefits and risks which he may face. He evidently is concerned about confronting abuse, even humiliation, from some Philippine oppositionists in the U.S. He recognizes that his visit will stimulate an outpouring of publicity about the Philippines in the U.S. press and he is skeptical that there will be much favorable coverage from the media."[3]

The regime countered as best as it could. During the first year of martial law, it ran colorful multipage spreads in influential U.S. business magazines such as *Fortune* and *Business Week*. The message: there was a new, much better investment climate in the country, and it was a safe tourist destination. Over the years, the Philippine campaign messages crystallized around the following points:

- the opposition espouses terrorism and violence;
- they are cowardly by attacking the Philippines from the safety of another country;
- they are sycophants of America;
- they live in luxury in America;
- they are hypocritical and have bad manners;
- the American media assist the opposition by slandering the Marcos government; this is sometimes done unwittingly, sometimes through ignorance, but usually through vindictiveness;
- the anti-Marcos groups, being part of world-wide Communism and sworn enemies of all democracies, exist to overthrow the rightful government of the Philippines.[4]

Because a large part of the opposition attacks, such as the war medals and the Maharlika exposés, targeted Marcos's personal character, the regime constructed a counteracting image: "that he is a strong leader as demonstrated by his subduing of Philippine violence; he is president independent of America; he saved and restored the country with martial law; he is destined to fulfill the greatness of the Filipino people."[5] At no time were these messages more fully heralded than during the state visit of Marcos to the United States in September 1982 at the invitation of President Reagan. For this visit, his first in sixteen years, the government went all out to counter any negative publicity. "Newspapermen, government media personnel, advertising executives and local leaders with connections in Washington and New York have already left to help prepare things," columnist Doroy Valencia wrote in the *Times Journal*.[6] Including public relations men borrowed from major Philippine corporations, a large advance party was dispatched to pave the way for the visit. Helping out were U.S.-based public relations firms hired specifically for the visit.[7] Aquino said that more than seven hundred people, including two hundred members of the Philippine press, traveled for the state visit at government expense.[8]

Press coverage was extensive during the fifteen-day visit. The Nixon, Ford, and Carter administrations, uneasy about Marcos's human rights record and conscious of Congress's inclination to reduce aid as a result, had not extended any invitations to Marcos during the ten-year period after the declaration of martial law. Reagan, who was less than two years into his presidency, now signaled that Philippine-U.S. relations were entering a new phase. That theme was reflected in the press coverage. The major TV networks, newspapers, and magazines covered his appearances before the National Press Club and the United Nations, and in meetings with congressional committees.[9] The accounts were objective, reported the *Filipino Chronicle*, a Washington, D.C.-based weekly, "except for a few that remained critical. But on the whole, said an Embassy official, the visit was not only successful, fruitful and exceeded expectations but was also a media success."[10] Asked Joseph McCallus, a scholar of media studies:

> Was the propaganda initiative successful? From the privileged position of this writer, it appeared to be so. Through the kindness of the Philippine Embassy . . . I was able to view the entire state visit on videotape. It would be difficult not to be impressed with the welcoming ceremonies, the "fire-fly" dinner in the White House garden, and the superb oratorical skills of President Marcos. Still more impressive were the images of

the Filipinos of Honolulu, of the West Coast, and of Washington: the hundreds, maybe thousands of smiling, cheering faces with Philippine flags and "Ako Ay Pilipino" [I am a Filipino] tee-shirts. Their obvious support of the president was a clear indication of the skill and success of the propaganda campaign.[11]

The *Filipino Chronicle* was a new arrival among the Filipino publications serving the northeast region. Only two years old during the Marcos visit, the *Chronicle* and the *Filipino Reporter*, a New York City–based weekly founded in 1972, favored the government. The *Reporter* circulated mostly in the city but also counted readers in the neighboring state of New Jersey. The *Chronicle* described itself as the "first Filipino-American Fortnightly in Metropolitan Washington D.C." In 1981, it reported a circulation of five thousand. As the only English-language D.C.-based publication for Filipinos in the area, it took on the job of telling the good news about the state visit. It devoted eleven of the twenty pages in its September 30, 1982, issue to the visit. In one of its 1983 issues, in a feature describing "deep internal dissention that has wracked MFP in recent years," it brought up the financial problems of the *Philippine News*, the weekly based in San Francisco, California. It called the *News* the "mouthpiece" of the MFP.[12]

Started by Filipino journalist Alex Esclamado in 1961 as the *Manila Chronicle*, the *Philippine News* grew to be the largest English-language Filipino newspaper, with a national circulation of forty thousand in the 1980s.[13] It had bureaus in major cities, with copies available in Filipino grocery stores and other outlets. If the *Chronicle* looked upon the *News* as a competitor, there was no comparison between the two. Not only had the *Philippine News* been around much longer, but it had built a loyal readership with news from the homeland at a time before the internet. Nonpartisan in its political views, but leaning toward conservatism, it expanded its base from the second generation of older immigrants to the third wave of newly arrived immigrants who were still hungry for homeland news. When martial law arrived, this desire turned to intense yearning. The newspaper responded by rehashing controlled press accounts from Manila. Not until April 1975 did Esclamado call on his readers to take a stand on martial law. In an editorial, he wrote:

> It is our view that the element of fear . . . was used effectively to intimidate the Filipinos in America into silence . . . Is the *Philippine News* then encouraging the Filipinos in America to come out in the open and express their views against the Marcos government?

Yes. Because we are cognizant of the fact that, rather than harm our people, this would be the best and most expeditious way to alleviate the plight of our countrymen . . .

The longer we in America who are free remain silent, the longer our people will suffer.[14]

Guilt, he hoped, would conquer fear.

Thereafter, practically every issue carried a negative feature about the Manila regime. The newspaper gave Steve Psinakis, one of the most outspoken U.S.-based critics of Marcos, a weekly column. In November 1975, Esclamado officially joined the MFP. He wrote that the regime had become so alarmed at the relentless crescendo of negative news that it had pressured the *News*'s advertisers to stop advertising, cutting off some $50,000 a year in revenues, mostly from travel agencies doing business between the United States and Manila. He also accused Marcos agents of repeatedly offering to buy the *News* at progressively increasing amounts. They offered, he said, $2 million in 1977, $5 million in 1979, and $12 million in 1981.[15]

The dominant position of the *Philippine News* so distressed Manila that "a few Ilocanos with American wives [wanted] to start a newspaper in the U.S. which would feature pro-Marcos material." The idea was relayed to the then U.S. ambassador to the Philippines, Richard Murphy, who advised Marcos, to the "unhappiness" of Mrs. Marcos, that such a "subterfuge" venture "would inevitably come to light, if for no other reason than as a result of investigative efforts by Marcos critics in the States. This would be counter-productive and embarrassing to both our governments."[16]

Another enemy that the *News* considered as evil as Marcos was the KDP's publication *Ang Katipunan*. To Esclamado, the KDP's advocacy of a Maoist violent revolution to overthrow Marcos would replace one dictatorship with another. "KDPs are Communists!" he exclaimed in large type in a 1979 issue. *Ang Katipunan* responded:

We find it hard to believe that anyone in the Filipino community . . . would be at all surprised or shocked at the "news" that the KDP actively supports the National Democratic Front, the NPA [New People's Army] and the CPP [Communist Party of the Philippines]. Alex Esclamado for one has known this for years. Ironically it is Esclamado and not the KDP who has tried to keep our work and politics a "secret" from the Philippine community. For quite some time, the *Philippine News* has intentionally distorted the news in order to deny or downplay the active and leading role of the KDP in many progressive activities and struggles in the Filipino community.[17]

In New York City, home to the largest concentration of Filipinos on the East Coast, the weekly English-language *Filipino Reporter* echoed the views of the Marcos government.[18] It did not publish a steady diet of pro-government propaganda, affecting a posture of nonpartisan objectivity. But its editorials and commentaries made it clear where its loyalties lay. It relied on dispatches from the government's Philippine News Agency (PNA) to deliver the more hard-hitting items against the exile opposition. For example, in 1982, it published a PNA analysis of the state of the U.S.-based opposition groups' nine-year campaign against the government. It laid out the following points:

- Washington's attitude, with a newly installed president, Ronald Reagan, had changed for the better, "resulting in widespread disillusion in the ranks" of the opposition groups;
- The "lifting of martial law has robbed the opposition of a vital weapon for their continued existence";
- "Recent press conferences staged by Filipino leftists . . . did not attract any of the correspondents of major papers";
- "There is a growing feeling in the ranks of Washington journalists that they are now being dragged by the opposition in their propaganda war";
- The MFP is "in disarray because it does not see eye-to-eye with the policy of Aquino and others joining with the MNLF or the Communist groups."

The report warned that the leftists would resort to violent means and that the FBI had been instructed "to infiltrate such groups and possibly start a crackdown on them."[19]

Growing fear on the part of Filipino immigrants that such actions had been set in motion and would intensify was most likely the reason for the small turnout of oppositionists at the events to welcome Marcos during his September 1982 state visit. But no such unease was evident among the opposition groups at a gathering a month before the visit. On one of those rare occasions when the disparate groups managed to band together for a common cause, ten groups organized into an Ad Hoc Coalition to Oppose the Marcos Visit. They met on the afternoon of August 30, 1982, on Manhattan's East Side on the fourth floor of the UN Plaza. "Snacks will be served," said the invitation to "An After-Office-Hours Meeting." And indeed a sumptuous spread of hors d'oeuvres on a table welcomed the participants, obviously the work of volunteers, cooked up in the kitchens of homes and apartments. On another table, literature spilled to the edges.

Multicolored flyers, brochures, newsletters, petitions—a whirlwind of words against a multitude of terrible things spawned by martial law: the extradition treaty, greedy multinational companies, poverty, malnutrition, militarization, Imelda Marcos's avarice. And taped on the walls were a profusion of posters denouncing the evils of the regime. There were also souvenirs for sale: greeting cards fashioned by political detainees and "Pinoy Ako" (I Am a Filipino) T-shirts.

The list of speakers included the more prominent faces of the opposition—Benigno Aquino, Raul Manglapus, Heherson Alvarez, Charito Planas. Attendees, mostly Filipinos, reflected the diverse mix represented by the Filipino population of New York City. Marcos's twelve-day itinerary featured several appearances in the city, for which the Ad Hoc Committee needed to mobilize. A dinner reception would be hosted by the Philippine-American Chamber of Commerce at the Waldorf-Astoria Hotel in Manhattan on September 20; there were to be receptions hosted by the Council on Foreign Relations the next day at its office on the East Side and in the Waldorf, as well as an address to the United Nations General Assembly at noon on September 22.

According to the 1980 city census, there were 23,810 Filipinos living in New York City, about 10 percent of the city's Asian population and 3.3 percent of its total population. Mostly white-collar workers in the service professions—in health care, law, engineering, and finance—they were generally uninterested in the city's political affairs. The leaders of the Filipino nurses' and doctors' organizations were quoted as saying that their members were "neutral" regarding Marcos, more concerned with their careers than with homeland politics. Not as geographically clustered into a Manilatown as were other Asians in the city, they were difficult to reach. These factors, as well as fear generated by the tight security, produced a low turnout, about one hundred, at the Waldorf-Astoria demonstration, offset by the volume of their noise. Outside the UN building on First Avenue, about fifty people were waving flags and banners—"Down with the U.S.-Marcos Dictatorship," said one. Overhead, a small plane, chartered by the committee and escorted by two police helicopters, trailed a sign reading "Stop Marcos."

There were similar signs hoisted by about one hundred demonstrators at Lafayette Park during the Philippine president's arrival in Washington, D.C., on September 16. They were clearly outnumbered by nearly one thousand pro-Marcos Filipinos "bused in from as far away as Norfolk, Virginia, lured with promises of free food, free lodging, and entertainment (provided by dancers brought in from the Philippines)," wrote *New York Times* reporter Raymond Bonner in his book *Waltzing with a Dictator*.[20]

He added that in the weeks before Marcos's arrival, there had been picnics for Filipino-Americans in five American cities, including Alexandria, Virginia (close to Washington, D.C.), and San Francisco, costing an estimated $410,000. Altogether, at least $5 million, and perhaps as much as $20 million, was spent on the state visit. The *New York Times* described the pomp and panoply of the arrival ceremonies as "one of the most carefully orchestrated events of its kind Washington has seen . . . it easily could have been scripted by Cecil B. De Mille."[21]

While the exile oppositionists were outclassed and certainly outspent by the Marcos government's public relations apparatus, they were not outmaneuvered. Amnesty International had released a copy of their report "Human Rights Violations in the Philippines" and published an advertisement of its findings in the *New York Times* on September 17, timing its release to coincide with the state visit.[22] The report documented extrajudicial executions, torture, arbitrary arrests and detentions, and political imprisonment. The opposition reprinted the ad in a leaflet and distributed it by the hundreds at three of the Marcos events in New York City—the Waldorf-Astoria dinner, the Council on Foreign Relations reception, and the United Nations address.

The Amnesty report struck a nerve with Marcos. "I come to the United States and what do I get? I get a confrontation with a supposed report from Amnesty International. I've never seen this in my life. Is that fair? And yet I am confronted with it here in the United States. It's not fair. Why didn't they confront me with it when I was in the Philippines and ready to meet with them on this matter?" he asked during a nationwide television interview on September 22 with anchorman Ted Koppel of ABC News's *Nightline*. Amnesty International in fact had tried several times to present him with their findings from a seventeen-day survey in November 1981 and wrote repeatedly to Philippine defense officials, all to no avail. On an earlier television network broadcast of NBC's *Meet the Press* on September 19, Marcos had been questioned about the report, and he had retorted that it was "sloppy reporting . . . I admit that some of these are correct and we punished some of those men." How many? During the same program, he remarked: "There are now pending in court more than oh, I would say about 500 cases of officers and men who have been charged with abuse. We have since 1972 to the present kicked out, dishonorably discharged from the Armed Forces about 7,000 men, among others." That was a staggering number by any measure, and attests to the rampant scale of the abuses.

Reunion Dinner of the Movement for a Free Philippines, Manila Mandarin Hotel, June 19, 1986. From left: Bonifacio Gillego, Mrs. Teresita Taca, Raul Manglapus, President Corazon Aquino, Arturo Taca, Mrs. Pacita Manglapus, Gaston Ortigas.

Manoling Maravilla, chairperson of the MFP's New York City chapter, demonstrates September 16, 1982, in front of the White House in Washington, D.C., during the state visit of President Marcos.

Demonstration and rally in Washington, D.C., 1983.

Conference sponsored by the Ninoy Aquino Movement, 1984, in Lincolnwood, Illinois.
From left: Heherson Alvarez, Steve Psinakis, unidentified person, Mrs. Priscilla Psinakis,
and U.S. civil rights activist Jesse Jackson.

State visit of President Ferdinand Marcos to the United States in September 1982.
From left: Marcos, President Ronald Reagan, Mrs. Imelda Marcos.

Meetings held September 17, 1982, in Washington, D.C., to counter Marcos's visit.
Left: Benigno Aquino at the podium. *Right:* Raul Manglapus.

THAT THE WORLD MAY KNOW

MOVEMENT FOR A FREE PHILIPPINES

No todos dormieron o pretendieron dormir en los dias oscuros de nuestra patria

Not everyone slept or pretended to sleep in the dark days of our country

—Jose Rizal, Philippine National Hero executed by Spain in 1896

On September 2, 1973, a year after the destruction of Philippine democracy, the Movement For A Free Philippines (MFP) which was launched last May in New York City, met in Washington, D.C. to forge itself into a national organization.

Its membership includes Filipinos, Americans, Canadians and men and women of other nationalities who are committed to work peacefully for the return of constitutional rule to the Republic of the Philippines.

TO THE FILIPINOS IN THE U.S.

MFP reminds President Ferdinand Marcos that his term of office expires at noon of December 30, 1973 as set by the 1935 Constitution, the only valid charter for the Republic.

If he should insist on clinging to the Presidency beyond that date, then he becomes not only the despotic dictator that he is but also a flagrant usurper.

Already he has violated the Constitution and the will of the people by declaring martial law on false excuses, suppressing civil rights, imprisoning thousands of innocent citizens whose only crime was to disagree with his policies, abolishing the Congress, cancelling the 1973 national elections, prostituting the Constitutional Convention and replacing the secret ballot plebiscite on the new Constitution with farcial "citizens assemblies" to justify his proclamation of his dictatorship.

MFP asks President Marcos not to compound these misdeeds with a constitutional crisis after December 30, 1973.

TO THE AMERICAN PEOPLE

Behind the deceptive facade of order and cleaner streets, President Marcos has substituted an explosive instability for the original stable, if imperfect, democratic system, by plugging the outlets for free expression and governing without successor. The resulting pent-up tensions may anyday explode and suck America with her large military and business presence into a prolonged and agonizing conflict as frustrating as Vietnam.

MFP is heartened and strongly supports the Abourezk amendment (Amendments No. 462 and 463) to the For-

eign Assistance Act of 1973 which prohibit: (1) providing aid to any country for police, prisons, internal intelligence or the maintenance of security forces; and (2) U.S. aid to any country which practices the internment or imprisonment of its citizens for political purposes.

MFP also supports the conclusion and recommendation of the report, recently declassified, of the U.S. Senate Appropriations Committee Delegation to Southeast Asia in January 1973 which states that "The Delegation is concerned at the growing trend toward authoritarian government in the Philippines. The United States should be careful to avoid any impression that its aid is helping to stifle dissent or impose authoritarian rule on the Filipino people."

MFP appeals to the U.S. Senators and Congressmen, and U.S. government agencies concerned, and to the American people, to support these amendments and recommendation in order to help restore democracy to the Philippine Republic, once so tenderly considered the foster child of America.

TO THE PEOPLE OF THE PHILIPPINES

MFP announces that an organization — the Filipino Freedom Fighters — has been formed in the Philippines with aims similar to ours. In its ranks are Filipinos of all classes, including some officers and men of the armed forces.

Both the MFP and the Filipino Freedom Fighters draw vigor and inspiration from each other, aware that they are resourceful allies in the same struggle.

The Filipino Freedom Fighters disseminated all over the Philippines on September 22, 1973 an open letter to President Marcos that seeks his compliance with the constitutional deadline of December 30, 1973. It is a reminder that the steps for an orderly return to democratic rule be initiated soon in order to spare our country the chaos of a constitutional breakdown.

Filipinos, Americans, Canadians, friends from everywhere —our unity will give us strength, our strength will defy all threats, our movement will yet recover for our prostrate people the liberties which are their heritage from their history and from their God.

Officers of the MFP: President, Hon. Raul S. Manglapus; Exec. Vice Pres., Dr. Renato Rosas: Sec.-General, J. Fuentecilla; Treasurer, Dr. Alfredo Arriola; Auditor, Antonio Valls, Regional Coordinators: East—Antonio Valls; Mid-west—Dr. Norberto Portugal West—Antonio Garcia. Regional Representatives to the Policy Board: East—Hon. Meharion Alvarez: Mid-west—Marc Crudo: West—Hon. Ruperto Baliao; Committee chairpersons: Socio political action—Ruby von Oxyen; Finance—Dr. Edgardo Espiritu; Information—Antonio Garcia; Research & Documentaton—Gerald Drummond; Education & Organization—Jun Atienza; Special Projects—Charlie Avila; Honorary Adviser Hon. Salvador Araneta.

Address all inquiries to: Movement For a Free Philippines, P. O. Box 568 Madison Sq. Station, New York, N.Y. 10010. Contributions are welcome.

Paid For by Filipino Citizens in America

Advertisement announcing the formation of the Movement for a Free Philippines, *New York Times*, September 27, 1973.

The Washington Post

February 26, 1986

Jubilation From Oxon Hill to Seattle

At Embassy and in Streets, Filipinos Hail 'Kalayaan'—Freedom

By Saundra Saperstein
and Eugene L. Meyer
Washington Post Staff Writers

To the blaring Motown sound of "Dancing in the Streets," a jubilant group of Filipino Americans danced outside the Philippine Embassy yesterday, guzzling frosty pink champagne, shouting "Kalayaan," which means freedom, and proclaiming, as one man said, that "victory champagne never tasted better."

Longtime opponents of Philippine President Ferdinand Marcos spoke with sweetness in their voices of newfound democracy in their homeland, and a priest thanked God "for removing the last roadblock to freedom." But there were also stern demands for new Philippine President Corazon Aquino to free political prisoners and an admonition for the Reagan administration not to grant political asylum to Marcos.

Throngs of pro-Aquino Filipinos here and around the nation celebrated the end of the two-decade Marcos era, which came to an abrupt close when Marcos fled the presidential palace in Manila yesterday. The event set off a flurry of parties and demonstrations.

There was a victory mass in Denver, a rally in Chicago, a "celebration picket" at Seattle's Philippine consulate and several gatherings near the United Nations in New York. There was a bittersweet moment of tears combined with shouts of joy outside the Newton, Mass., home where the new president's husband, Benigno Aquino, lived in exile before he returned to the Philippines in 1983 and was assassinated.

In the Washington area, it was also a day that highlighted some of the divisions within the Filipino community. At the embassy, some employes watched warily as Aquino supporters were allowed in for an impromptu victory celebration in the ornate, now empty, office of the former ambassador, where above the mantel is a large blank space that once held a portrait of Marcos. The celebrants drank champagne and took apart a paper shredder in

BY DUDLEY M. BROOKS—THE WASHINGTON POST
Outside Philippine Embassy, 80-year-old Pura Castrense flashes victory smile.

the office, later handing over its contents to a transition team named by the Aquino government.

In southern Prince George's County, where the largest concentration of local Filipinos lives, two priests talked of the often submerged political differences among their parishioners at St. Columba Church in Oxon Hill.

"We don't say anything from the pulpit, but people have been giving out literature outside the masses," said the Rev. John de Wan, who has watched the community grow during his 18 years at the church. About 500 of those attending each Sunday mass at St. Columba are Filipino, and some estimate that as many as 10,000 Filipinos live in southern Prince George's area.

For the last three years, de Wan's assistant pastor has been a Filipino, the Rev. Fidel de Ramos. "There are so many elements in our parish," said de Ramos. "Marcos even has a distant relative here.

"Actually, I'm happy for the new government and I'm happy for the peaceful transition," de Ramos said.

By and large, both ministers said, political differences have been held beneath the surface. "I don't see any bad blood," said de Ramos, who has stayed publicly neutral. "They all still talk to each other."

But there were divisions, even within families. David Valderrama, a Philippine-born Prince George's County probate judge, said his broth-

er was Philippine ambassador to Australia and was recently reassigned to New York to be an official spokesman for the Marcos government.

"He was on CNN [Cable News Network] talking for Marcos, while I was in Lafayette Park speaking against Marcos," said Valderrama, who came here in 1961 to study and became a judge in December. "It's been a very, very delicate situation."

But for the most part, it was a day for coming together both here and around the country. On a Houston radio station, Philippine consul Rodolfo Severino said he felt "relief that this whole thing has been settled relatively peacefully." He said he felt "compassion" for Corazon Aquino, adding, "She's got a very difficult job ahead of her."

Some pro-Aquino leaders praised the Reagan administration. Crispin R. Aranda, an anti-Marcos leader who is now a New Jersey publisher, said, "With the way the events developed, the Reagan administration handled it with a plus overall."

In Washington, celebrants attended a mass at St. Matthew's Cathedral, then streamed back across 17th Street to the embassy's front door on Massachusetts Avenue NW as friendly motorists honked their horns and waved. During the rally earlier, Jon Melegrito, a longtime local leader of the anti-Marcos forces, had proclaimed, "This is now our embassy," with heavy emphasis on the word "our."

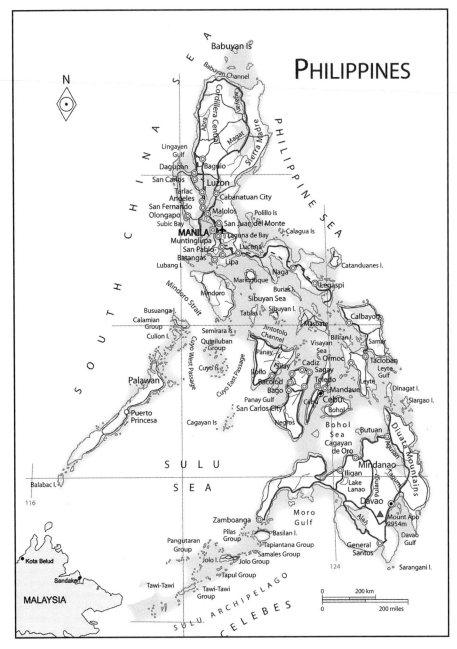

Prominent Filipino political exiles escaped the Philippines by island-hopping the Sulu Archipelago (bottom), then sought refuge in Malaysia before making their way to the United States.

CHAPTER 10

Reviving the Opposition
Arrival of an Exile Hero

In the New York City borough of Queens, in the Hollis neighborhood, there is a triangular cement island on a street at 184th Place, south of Hillside Avenue. On one side of the triangle is a hair salon; on the opposite side is a pharmacy. Along this street are rows of modest two-story wooden homes, similar in appearance, with small front lawns fenced with iron grilles. At one end of the triangle, atop two tall poles, Philippine and American flags flutter in the wind. Between them is a granite tombstone-like marker with an inscription reading:

> Benigno S. Aquino, Jr.
> Man's Sense of Justice Demands Democracy.
> Man's Injustice Makes It Necessary.

This marker honors a Filipino political exile known to most if not all of the Filipinos who live on the street. In fact, the site was chosen because census figures say that there is a dense population of Filipinos in this neighborhood. Aquino, better known by his nickname "Ninoy," arrived in Dallas, Texas, from the Philippines on May 8, 1980, for heart bypass surgery. He returned to Manila on August 21, 1983, only to be gunned down as he descended the plane's stairs at the airport.

When Aquino arrived in Texas, he had spent the preceding seven years and seven months in a military prison. Caught in the dragnet of martial law mass arrests in 1982, he was among the first political prisoners to be rounded up. He certainly was the most famous. In the annals of Philippine political history, his ascent to prominence was stellar. At the age of twenty-two, he was elected the youngest mayor of his hometown, Concepcion, in Tarlac province on the northern island of Luzon. Opponents protested that the minimum age requirement for the position was twenty-three. Two years later, a court unseated him. At twenty-six, he staged a comeback as the youngest elected vice governor of the province; four years later, he won the governorship, victorious in all seventeen towns. At thirty-four years of age, he was the youngest senator elected to the national Congress, the lone opposition Liberal Party candidate amid the election sweep of the incumbent Nacionalista Party of President Marcos.

During the next four years, Aquino stood in the Senate as the severest critic of Marcos. At the next Senate elections in 1971, his party won six of the eight contested seats. That positioned him as the presidential candidate most likely to replace Marcos, whose third and last term would end in 1973. Martial law dashed that possibility. He refused to take part in his trial before a military commission and went on a forty-day hunger strike to protest what he considered a sham trial. He was found guilty of subversion, illegal possession of firearms, and murder. The sentence: death by firing squad. While in jail, he was allowed to run for a Manila seat against Imelda Marcos in the 1978 elections for the interim Legislative Assembly. Campaigning from his cell as the head of LABAN, he lost. All twenty-one Manila seats were taken by Marcos's party. Manila residents turned out into the streets, banging on pots and pans, tooting car horns, and chanting "Laban! Laban!" (Fight! Fight!) to let Aquino "hear" of their support for him.

While Aquino was in jail, he had a heart attack. Concerned with the consequences for his regime should Aquino die incarcerated, Marcos temporarily released him for medical treatment abroad. His arrival in the United States galvanized the Filipino opposition movement. Not only did he have an impressive record of public service, but he had endured a long prison sentence, isolated from his wife and family; he was a sworn enemy of Marcos; he had an unbroken spirit; and he was a proven fighter and a leader. "Activity picked up when Ninoy arrived. Everybody was euphoric. The superstar," said Jose "Joey" Ortiz, an MFP member. "There was a qualitative change. I told him we must carry on the campaign. The Americans are telling us that you are in no position to take power, that you do not have the clout. They were comparing us with the Left. If Marcos falls, the only alternative is the Left," Heherson Alvarez, an MFP officer told him.[1]

Aquino had promised Marcos that he would not speak out against him while in the United States, but he broke that promise in his first public speech. At the Asia Society on August 4, 1980, he warned of dire things to come unless the regime changed its ways:

> I have been told of plans for the launching of a massive urban guerrilla warfare where buildings will be blown up, and corrupt presidential cronies and cabinet ministers assassinated along with military officers who have engaged in wanton and rampant tortures of political prisoners. There are plans to disrupt tourism. Also to kidnap the children of corrupt aliens who have exploited our people mercilessly and who have profited immensely from their Palace connections . . . The guerrillas are well-educated, articulate young men and women who have patiently studied the latest tactics in urban warfare. If there is such a thing as the Light A Fire Movement, let me assure you Mr. Marcos it will not be the last. More are coming, better trained and better prepared . . . This is no idle talk.[2]

Marcos dismissed the threat. In a speech on August 8, he said: "today the media is full of lurid tales about somebody who is supposed to be mounting a rebellion against the Philippines. Such a fantastic tale is so stupid, so ridiculous that I cannot dignify it by a comment . . . We should instead not only ask [the doctors] to cure his heart but cure his mind as well."[3]

Less than two weeks later, on August 22, nine explosions rocked Manila, causing minor damage and injuring two people. The April 6 Liberation Movement, a reference to the April 6 street "noise barrage" of the last elections, issued a two-page manifesto, saying in part: "This is only the beginning. We have decided to use force against a repressive regime that has refused to listen to reason . . . Today bombs have exploded in the business establishments owned by Marcos cronies and allies. Tomorrow we shall strike again."[4] They did strike again, on September 12. A number of people were injured in the bombings, and an American woman was killed while shopping at Rustan's Supermarket in Makati, Manila. On October 4, more bombs hit three big hotels.

The A6LM advised the delegates to an upcoming convention of the American Society of Travel Agents (ASTA) to cancel their October 20 meeting in Manila. "We ask you to sympathize with our cause," its letter said. The government and the FBI assured the ASTA that the chances of an incident were small. Extra security had been added, with three thousand personnel assigned to protect the convention site. But the meeting went on as scheduled. Marcos himself assured them that "the nightmare . . . of fear and apprehension" in the Philippines under martial law was "past and gone."[5] So when the five thousand delegates at the International Convention Center heard an explosion while they were watching a noisy slide show of Admiral George Dewey's 1898 flotilla blasting the Spanish fleet in Manila Bay, they thought that it was part of the sound effects. But it was a real bomb, and it had exploded barely fifty feet from Marcos. Eighteen delegates, eleven of them from abroad, were hurt. The ASTA canceled the public sessions, and many delegates fled to their hotels, packed their bags, and flew out of the country.

The next day, the *Bulletin Today* reported arrest orders for thirty suspects. Heading the list were Aquino, Manglapus, and Osmena. Others who were identified as MFP members were Alvarez, Psinakis, Gillego, Planas, Raul Daza, Antonio Daza, Eugenio Lopez Jr., Danny Lamila, Narciso Manzano, and Orly Candari, all living in the United States. Six KDP members, also in the U.S., were listed. Senator Jovito Salonga was served his arrest order at the Medical Center in Manila, where he was confined for asthma. Later he was transferred to a prison cell at the Fort Bonifacio army camp.[6]

In an interview with the *Washington Post*, Defense Minister Juan Ponce Enrile described the bombers as belonging to a "violence prone faction of an older Christian activist organization that embraces both Roman Catholic and Protestant church members and includes besides students and workers, a number of doctors, lawyers and engineers. There is a moral quality to their movement. Our people are basically very religious and religious people have a strong influence on the people. It is not large yet but has the potential for becoming a large force if we do not stop them."[7]

Mark Thompson, a political scientist who interviewed some Light-A-Fire and A6LM members, wrote that "from his jail cell Aquino helped direct and organize the LAF" and that Aquino and Psinakis also supported the A6LM. "The A6LM was to be larger, better equipped and more professionally trained than the LAF, but it would also try to minimize the loss of life in its symbolic acts of terror. Bombings were meant to provoke protests, not to substitute for them." In discussing this strategy with Gillego and Ortigas, according to Thompson, Manglapus "questioned the rationale for an insurrectional strategy. He argued that without an extensive network of supporters or a mass base, the opposition's efforts to overthrow Marcos would fail as certainly as the LAF had, when it did not spark a mass uprising as the bombers wanted. Instead, he recommended trying to broaden the opposition's appeal by developing a progressive ideology for a new political party in preparation for future elections."[8]

Psinakis thought otherwise. Aquino told him that Imelda Marcos was in New York City and that he had met with her on December 16. She had told Aquino that she wanted to speak with Psinakis. Initially reluctant to meet with her, Psinakis decided that her desire to see him must have something to do with the bombings. He surmised that she was in town to seek some kind of accommodation with the U.S.-based opposition. For one thing, Pope John Paul II was scheduled to come to Manila the following year, and an ASTA-style incident would be disastrous to her husband's image. In other words, Psinakis concluded that the bombings had worked in shaking up Marcos. So he flew from San Francisco to Mrs. Marcos's suite at the Waldorf-Astoria Hotel on Park Avenue in New York City. What followed was a four-hour verbal duel, polite but strained, that ended with an agreement for a "moratorium" on any violence while Marcos worked out the process of lifting martial law. As it turned out, he never did. Psinakis's allies in Manila, who had held off on any more bombing, said that he had been duped.

Nor was Manglapus particularly happy about Psinakis's meeting with Mrs. Marcos. In a letter to him, he wrote: "I have received a substantial number of calls from our officers and members in the MFP . . . appealing to me to make a clear statement, if not to the press, at least for circulation among our members. They appear to be confused, not so much by you seeing Imelda, but by the report that MFP top officers saw her."[9] Alvarez also met with Mrs. Marcos on December 20. Psinakis told Manglapus that he went not to represent the MFP but on his own. "Yes, it's hard to separate me from MFP since I am indeed a high officer and quite active but on the other hand, I, through Presy's family, have had a long history of personal involvement with the Marcoses and my family's relationship is quite unique," he explained.[10] Psinakis is married to Eugenio Lopez's daughter Presy. During pre–martial law times, Presy and Imelda mingled socially. Psinakis added that Aquino was "strongly in favor of my seeing Imelda." Manglapus was adamant about sticking to a policy that top MFP officers, including himself, should never meet with high-level Marcos officials. He was concerned that any publicity from a meeting would be distorted by the Manila-controlled press into a propaganda trap.

At the MFP's eighth annual convention in Detroit, Michigan, August 29–31, 1980, Manglapus offered Aquino the presidency of the organization. Aquino declined, saying that he did not want to be identified with any opposition group—not yet, anyway—but eventually he forged connections with MFP officers, among them Psinakis, Charles Avila, and Taca. After his surgery, he moved to Boston, where for the next three years he was a research fellow and lecturer at Harvard University and a research fellow at the Center for International Affairs at the Massachusetts Institute of Technology. From his Boston base, he received updates on Philippine developments, maintained links with members of the exile and nonexile opposition groups, gave interviews to the media, received visitors, and went out on meeting and speaking tours. His wife, Corazon, and daughter, Kris (who was an infant when her father went to jail and eight years old when he was released), were able to join him in Massachusetts. It was there, on December 18, 1980, that he composed a letter to Marcos, restating his conversation with Mrs. Marcos in New York and presenting his program for an orderly transition to democracy. Right afterward, he typed out a memorandum to the opposition leaders in Manila, all senators, detailing a step-by-step agenda for how they could work with Marcos in lifting martial law.

He never lost the desire to return home. He was feeling irrelevant and powerless in the United States. Said Corazon: "Throughout our three years in the United States, we were always aware that our life was temporary. Ninoy never ceased talking about returning to the Philippines . . . Ninoy believed that it was imperative for him to return our country to democracy before extreme forces were released that would make such a return impossible. I told Ninoy that Marcos would not listen to him, that the man is completely calloused. Ninoy said 'I will never forgive myself if I did not at least try.' When I heard this, I knew there was nothing I could do to stop him from returning."[11]

When a friend, the journalist Teodoro Locsin, tried to discourage him—"What will you gain? Suppose you are shot?"—Aquino replied: "Well, you know Teddy, the Spaniards made a mistake. If they had not recalled Rizal and shot him, he would have ended his life a mere exile. He would be nothing in our history . . . If they make a mistake of killing me or shooting me, they will make me a hero and they will lose and I will win."[12] Other reasons were advanced for his decision to return. Yossi Shain and Mark Thompson wrote that "Aquino calculated that he would only be imprisoned, a preferable situation to the growing sterility of exile politics."[13] Moreover, they claimed that both Aquino and Manglapus lost political influence when their respective parties in the Philippines merged with larger coalitions of parties that formed to oppose Marcos for the May 1984 legislative elections. Aquino wanted to reassert his leadership with his return. Thompson also speculated that Aquino "felt he had to return in order to persuade the U.S. government to back him and abandon Marcos."[14]

"Ninoy and I were in close touch," Manglapus recalled, "especially before his fateful departure. He often lamented to me that our countrymen were showing so much apathy. In his last call to me from San Francisco he reiterated to me colloquially his reason for going home: 'Mangugulo ako!' [I'll make trouble!] 'Ikaw na ang bahala dito sa America' [You take care of things here in America]."[15] The spark that Manglapus had hoped for was ignited by Aquino's death on August 21, 1983. Within three years after his return, that spark had spread across the country, firing up not the radicals, not the leftists, but the mass of previously apathetic citizens, who now launched the People Power revolution. But it was a slow three-year simmer until 1986, when Marcos fled the country.

Ten days after Aquino's murder, Filipinos in the U.S. watched televised images of the burial procession as his body was taken from the Santo Domingo Church to the Manila Memorial Park. The route through the city was thirty kilometers long. The procession lasted eleven hours. From the aerial views, it was estimated that two million people lined the route—an immense gathering of humanity that had never before been seen and probably will never be seen again in Manila's or Philippine history. It was a historic tribute to a martyr, for that was how the people viewed the circumstances of his murder.

Opposition groups in the United States realized that they could not match the scale of this great emotional outpouring. It would have been a monumental task to assemble a substantial throng for a centralized protest from a widely dispersed Filipino population. They did, however, organize memorials and Aquino-themed activities. The following list provides a sampling of those that were conducted in metropolitan New York City alone by the MFP and its allies:

August 21	A Requiem Mass at St. Joseph's Church in Manhattan on the day of the assassination, attended by 200 people. Television coverage was provided by the U.S. media.
August 22	The start of a six-day vigil in front of the Philippine consulate in Manhattan, with from 30 to 100 people in attendance at any given time. Six thousand signatures were collected on petitions.
August 26	A memorial service at the Holy Family Church in Manhattan. Among the speakers were Senator Edward Kennedy and Patricia Derian, the assistant secretary of state for human rights in the Jimmy Carter administration. An overflow crowd of 500 spilled out onto the sidewalk in front of the church.

August 31   A memorial service at the American Martyrs Church in Bayside, New York; 150 people attended.

September 2   A memorial service at St. Aedan's Church in Jersey City, attended by 1,000 people.

September 20 A memorial service at Holy Family Church in Manhattan, followed by an open forum. The speaker was Representative Stephen Solarz, chairman of the Subcommittee on Asian and Pacific Affairs of the House Committee on Foreign Affairs; 300 people attended.

October 14   A memorial service at Fordham University.

October 28   A rally in front of the White House to thank President Reagan for canceling a planned visit to Manila in the wake of the murder. With 700 participants, it was one of the largest MFP multichapter gatherings, attended by members from Detroit, Philadelphia, Virginia, Ohio, New York, and New Jersey. A busload of Justice for Aquino—Justice for All (Ja-Ja) members joined.

Similar activities were conducted by other MFP chapters, together with groups such as the KDP and FFP, in Chicago, San Francisco, Los Angeles, and Washington, D.C.

A larger than expected turnout by Filipinos at these events was attributed to the dramatic circumstances of Aquino's death and the U.S. media attention given to it. Moreover, Aquino's three-year stay in America had enhanced his anti-Marcos reputation. He was already a well-known personality before he arrived. For those who were still uneasy about getting into politics, attending a religious service was not an explicit political act. Still, traces of fear lingered in the minds of Filipino immigrants despite the emotional urge to respond. If the government could do this to someone like Aquino, they could do it to anyone. The heavy political overtones surrounding Aquino's death worried some Filipino communities. When Filipino parishioners heard that a memorial service was to be held at the Immaculate Conception Church in Jamaica Estates in Queens, a priest in the parish was informed about the political implications. The service was canceled. Dr. Orlando Apiado, an MFP officer for the New York region, was so incensed that he told the priest: "Father, you are being a hypocrite like Pontius Pilate washing your hands from this affair. I pity you. This man will end up to be a hero and a martyr for his people. There are a lot of Filipinos in this area. When a mafia leader dies, his body is brought to your Church."[16]

For the oppositionists, it was an opportunity to raise political consciousness and to tap into people's latent desire to become involved. New opposition groups emerged. Existing groups, which normally were difficult to get together for forums or discussion sessions, lent their names and urged their members to attend. Justice for Aquino—Justice for All was the first new group to emerge in New York City. Within weeks, its founder, Cris Abasolo, a lawyer, had lined up officers and coordinators across the country. They included a number of well-known names. Officers from established groups such as the MFP were invited to speak at the rallies and memorial services that Ja-Ja organized, creating confusion with their seeming endorsement of a competing group. In due time, Ja-Ja agreed to merge with the MFP.

In February 1984, Alvarez founded the Ninoy Aquino Movement (NAM) in San Francisco. Because of his close association with Aquino, the new group attracted a large number of followers, including MFP members. The MFP laid down a rule that its rank-and-file members were welcome to join, in the name of unifying democratic elements in the Filipino community, but its top officers could not accept leadership positions. NAM, said Alvarez, would concentrate on propagating Aquino's legacy, while the MFP would focus on lobbying. Prior to the establishment of these ground rules, charges were exchanged about membership poaching between the new and the established groups. Bitter feuds erupted between the leaders. Multipage letters threatened lawsuits. Critics warned that the clash of egos would shatter an already fragile unity. In a letter, an exasperated member, Jose Calderon, wrote: "It is a pity that we have to devote part of our precious time to settling intramurals . . . Our people still have much to learn. They can disagree without being disagreeable or nasty about it."[17]

Events marking Aquino's birthday and the anniversary of his death were used to gain members. More importantly, they became the springboard for political action (letters, telegrams) in support of the groups' congressional agendas. There was a surge of activities inspired by the assassination among the MFP chapters in October and November 1983. In California, for example, 150 people attended a meeting of the Salinas/Monterey chapter. A fundraising dinner sponsored by the Foster City chapter drew 120 people, while 200 attended a fundraising dinner in Chicago. MFP officers, especially Manglapus, took part in the events to help increase attendance. Manglapus's "star power" was put to good use during a one-week speaking tour in February 1984 in Los Angeles. He spoke at UCLA, the University of Southern California, Claremont College, and the Southwestern Law School. At the opening of the San Diego chapter, 700 people came to hear him. On February 23, 300 people attended his appearance at the World Affairs Council of Los Angeles.

With Aquino dead, Filipinos in America, as well as their relatives back home, sought answers to troubling questions: What now? Who would take his place as the main opposition leader? Was the Marcos government going to fall? Would the left (with their organized ideological base and armed allies) now be in a position to take advantage of the people's anger and frustration? One scenario that scared them was presented by the *Wall Street Journal*: "The extreme left is waiting on the sidelines. The minute they see the moderates are not getting anywhere, they'll move in" to fill the power vacuum.[18]

Having emphasized in the media and his speeches that the MFP supported only "moderate" means to return democracy to the Philippines, Manglapus now had to spell out specifics to a largely middle-class Filipino community wary about the use of violence. And in the light of the MFP's adoption of the "Armalite Resolution" justifying "force" when necessary, more questions arose. Most troubling of all—when would martial law end? Marcos "officially" lifted it in January 1981, partly to appease the U.S. Congress, which was threatening to cut off aid. But in reality his dictatorial powers remained intact. And despite the massive show of rage that pointed to government complicity in Aquino's murder, he resisted any relaxation of his rule. He had scheduled elections on May 14, 1984, to fill the 183 seats in the regular National Assembly. With no organized opposition, his KBL ruling party was expected to retain power as it had after the interim National Assembly elections in April 1978.

With less than six weeks before the elections, an extraordinary meeting took place in Hong Kong on April 4. Three former senators, the representative of a former president, and the brother of the slain Aquino sat down to "agree on a common action." One of the former senators, Jovito Salonga, like Manglapus was living in exile in the U.S. This was the first time that prominent oppositionists, inside and outside the Philippines, had gotten together.[19] The choice of Hong Kong as the meeting site carried historic undertones. It was there in 1897 that a group of Filipino intellectuals had formed a Central Revolutionary Committee to function as the Philippine government in exile. The Hong Kong Junta, as they were called, collected funds, food, and other provisions to support the anticolonial Filipino revolution against Spain and later the United States. The 1984 version of the Junta immediately agreed to urge their followers to boycott the May elections. Then they tackled the ultimate issue—what to do next beyond the boycott. They announced a preparatory committee to "lay the groundwork for a Transitory Government representing all sectors of our society": "the churches and church-related organizations, peasant and trade unions, farmers, workers, our Muslim brothers and other cultural communities, professionals, businessmen, intellectuals, teachers, employees, and conscience-stricken members of the Armed Forces." The committee would initially be composed of the six men at the Hong Kong meeting. The document they signed—"An Appeal for Unity and a Pledge of Solidarity"—urged all of these sectors to join together in "militant, non-violent mass action" against the Marcos regime.

At a press conference the next day, on April 5, former senator Lorenzo Tanada said that the transitory government would prepare for a plebiscite that "will approve or disapprove a form of government or a Constitution that will be submitted to them in a free election." He would not specify the forms that "mass action" should take. Manglapus noted, however, that "no country moves from dictatorship to democracy through the electoral process. The dictatorship must fall first. The very existence of a transitory government would help to forestall any possible coup if Marcos fell. What we are looking for is precisely the opposite to a military coup. We are asking for them to return to the barracks." The Appeal for Unity document made no mention of the United States. But at the press conference, the "signatories declared they would not tolerate the continued existence of United States military bases . . . and that foreign aid would be acceptable only if it did not serve the purpose of shoring up the Marcos government."[20]

Manglapus now had in his hands a document containing an answer to the insistent question: What now, with Aquino gone? He returned to the United States to start work on the campaign for a boycott of the election—to urge Filipino residents in the United States to tell their relatives and friends back home that the election of a regular National Assembly would not change things. Over the six-year term of the interim National Assembly elected in 1978, Marcos's KBL party (151 members out of 165) had strengthened the patronage system across the country. A Philippine publication, *Panorama* magazine, described the extent of its reach: "It has 71 governorships and 69 vice governorships out of a total of 73 provinces; 54 city mayors and 53 vice mayors out of 60 cities; 1,238 municipal mayorships out of 1,514 such posts. It has the Assembly under its full control, or rather the control of its KBL chief—Marcos. He is definitely the sun around which the KBL revolves and his power the source of the party's own."[21] Even if freely elected, the 1984 National Assembly would fall under the shadow of a 1973 constitutional provision that gave Marcos the power to overrule it. Indeed, over the lifetime of the 1978 Assembly, it had passed 450 laws. Over the same period, Marcos had issued 950 decrees that carried the force of law but were not passed by the Assembly.

The Hong Kong conference was the closest that Manglapus had come to setting foot on Philippine soil. In a meeting there in March 1983 with his closest associates from the Christian Social Movement, they talked about whether it was time for him to return home "regardless of risk and consequences." If so, the 1984 elections could be the most favorable opportunity. According to one estimate, the CSM had a mass base of one million potential supporters. They said there was a need for him to reassert his leadership of the organization and to consolidate it. His followers, he was told, felt the "growing irrelevance of exile leadership to the situation in the Philippines." They considered other factors as well: "the common people are neither aware nor appreciative of [Raul's] activities in the USA; traditional political leaders in the opposition are more aligned with Ninoy than [him]; 'if [Raul] desires to vie for national leadership, the longer [he] remains in the USA, the lesser [his]chances would be to be even considered as a serious contender.'"[22]

During Manglapus's first years in exile, emissaries with family connections were sent to convince him to return, promising no harm or harassment. In October 1976, the first of what he called "newspaper invitations" headlined an offer from Marcos for him and MFP associates to participate in that year's referendum. Knowing better, Manglapus shot back a reply: "The Philippines is my country. To return to it, I do not need your invitation nor your guarantees. I will go home in my own time."[23] The suggestions to return were also couched in other ways. A magazine in the Philippines asked: "But Raul, you are fighting out there [in the United States] and are not in the frontline with the troops [in the Philippines]. Shouldn't you be running in the next elections where the battleground is?" He replied: "Let us imagine myself going home. And let us assume that I will not be imprisoned nor will I be harmed, which by the way is not the opinion of some. But let us assume I will be safe. I run. I will be spending my time trying to prove myself the better candidate than somebody else in some district, maybe the First District of Rizal, rather than devoting myself and my leadership to bringing Marcos down. The one who will enjoy all of this is Marcos."[24]

CHAPTER 11

Reviewing the Decade

Adding Up the Losses and Wins

When MFP delegates assembled for a three-day conference in Illinois beginning on September 2, 1983, they chose a site owned by a religious order, the Society of the Divine Word (SVD), located in the Chicago suburb of Techny. The SVD has sent hundreds of missionaries overseas since 1909. The conference rooms were designed to showcase some of the countries where they were assigned. There was, for example, a Philippine room. One of the SVD's Filipino missionaries, Fr. Edicio de la Torre, had been in military detention in Manila for eight years, a political prisoner charged with rebellion by the Marcos government.

The MFP was marking its tenth year. It had a new chairman, Dr. Renato "Ato" Roxas, who, together with some other doctors, had founded the chapter in Detroit, Michigan, in 1973. He had been the assistant head of the Department of Anesthesia at the Children's Hospital of Michigan for the previous fourteen years. On the day Roxas was elected, May 14, 1983, Manglapus observed that since the organization's founding ten years earlier, it had reached "a level of maturity. As a result, more leaders developed from the Filipino community, greater initiatives were mobilized from the local levels to help the Movement."[1] In addition, its structure had been decentralized a year earlier, allowing its eight regions more autonomy from central control in Washington, D.C. Having been relieved of the organizational duties attendant to the office of chairman, Manglapus declared that he would concentrate on representing the MFP before the U.S. government, international organizations, and the various opposition groups in the Philippines. The *Manila Bulletin*, a pro-government newspaper, was quick to proclaim the event. It cited, without attribution, remarks from members about "disillusioned officers . . . weakening . . . diminishing financial support . . . a vehicle for his personal ambition."[2] The members had expected the distorted spin from a government-controlled publication.

There was a disconsolate mood to this anniversary gathering. Aquino had been assassinated barely a month earlier. The White House had submitted a five-year, $900 million bases "compensation package" for Congress to approve. An extradition treaty between the Philippines and the United States, signed in 1981, had been cleared by the relevant House and Senate committees and was on its way to the full chambers for floor debate. The U.S. media warned that Marcos might attempt to use it as a tool for persecution against his enemies in the United States. Over the previous year, a grand jury had been impaneled to look into the MFP, fulfilling a promise to Marcos by the new Reagan administration that it would start cracking down on his political enemies in the U.S.

It was time to analyze the record of their ten-year struggle. They agreed that the movement had earned recognition from the various audiences they had targeted—the Filipino community, the U.S. Congress, the media. The Filipino community, by and large, looked to them as a more acceptable organization than the leftist opposition groups. The MFP's many appearances before House and Senate committees and its close ties with several legislators from both U.S. political parties had strengthened its access to Congress and gained it some influential advocates. It had established valuable contacts in the media by providing them with useful information on developing their stories (the fake Marcos medals, the nonexistent Maharlika, and the Manhattan real estate acquired by Mrs. Marcos). Although it disagreed with the ideological focus of the other opposition groups, it had participated in their forums, rallies, and other public activities in the name of unity.

With respect to the MFP's organizational maturation, its acceptance of its members' differing views had been both an asset and a liability. In an internal memorandum, Tom Achacoso, a member, wrote:

> Pluralism was an important feature of MFP in order to accommodate the diversity of views of its members. Commitment to its goals ranged from total to segmental participation, from the "paper" variety to a vague restlessness about change. Many look on with interest but remain distant due to the more immediate needs and worries of day-to-day living. Crucial issues developed from the distinction between a powerful and

authoritative day-to-day leadership and the less routine and less regular membership. As a consequence, the MFP was required to stress action-now programs and dramatic activities with high visibility to heighten excitement and intensity, gain attention to the MFP programs, and bring in converts and reinforce partisans.[3]

The leftist Filipino opposition groups, in both the United States and the Philippines, concluded early on that the MFP was elitist, in that it was led by former Philippine politicians, intellectuals, and affluent community leaders. Its program to restore, by "moderate means," democracy in the Philippines would result in a return to old oligarchic structures. Voices in Washington warned about so-called "moderate" forces opposing Marcos. A new conservative Republican think tank that emerged after Reagan took office was described as one of the most influential in Washington, D.C. The Heritage Foundation claimed that 60 percent of the more than six thousand policy suggestions it had submitted to the White House in 1980 had been implemented. In addition to domestic and economic policies among its areas of research, the foundation prepared policy recommendations on Asian issues. It issued two "backgrounder" reports and a monograph on the Philippines. Identifying Manglapus as one of the leaders of the "moderate" opposition, a twelve-page backgrounder by A. James Gregor of the University of California at Berkeley concluded:

> The present "moderate" opposition to the Marcos government is manifestly anti-American by conviction, and however much their overt behavior might be modified by the realities of power, their commitment to the security of Southeast Asia and to a realistic policy of economic development for the region is, at best, questionable. The leadership of the anti-Marcos opposition has been so long inured to the "anti-imperialist" notions of the neo-Marxist left that it is unlikely that the U.S. can ever have confidence in its behavior.[4]

The Heritage Foundation made sure that its position papers reached the right people. They went to 8,000 political decision makers, including every member of Congress, 1,200 congressional staffers sorted by expertise, 900 members of the executive branch, and 3,500 journalists. If it was particularly successful, "it is partly because of its many ties to the administration . . . knowingly and at times brilliantly marketing its right-wing ideas for maximum impact," wrote the *Wall Street Journal*.[5] Gregor acknowledged that the exile opposition in the U.S. was "effective":

One reason for the heavy focus of attention by U.S. human rights activists on the Republic of the Philippines is probably the special responsibility Americans feel toward that nation. The Philippines was a colony for almost half a century, and Americans like to believe that, on its independence, it became a "showcase of democracy." Any departure from democracy appears a betrayal. But more important, perhaps, is the fact that there are between one half and one million ethnic Filipinos and naturalized Americans of Filipino origin resident in the United States. And the major Filipino opposition groups in exile are among the most vocal lobbies in Washington, reportedly capable of "exerting pressure on Congress out of proportion to their numbers." They have used the human rights issues very effectively.[6]

A nonpartisan view was expressed by the Congressional Research Service, a U.S. government agency that provides members of Congress with objective analysis of issues:

> Most Filipino groups in opposition to President Marcos have criticized U.S. assistance to the Philippines which they view as giving President Marcos the means to maintain authoritarian rule. Some of these opposition groups reside in the United States. Their numbers are relatively few, and they have only limited influence among the 900,000-member Philippine-American community. However, their lobbying efforts in the U.S. have contributed to the call for a review of U.S.-Philippine relations by some Members of Congress, some human rights groups, and others concerned with the consequences for the U.S. of instability in the Philippines.[7]

The briefing materials prepared by the U.S. State Department for Marcos's 1980 visit described the range of growing political opposition against him—from insurgents to church progressives. It added:

> The picture would be incomplete without noting the growing challenge of the anti-Marcos groups in the U.S. who are working energetically, especially on the Hill, to publicize Marcos' failings and block further military aid. The groups include some former Philippine politicians and scions-in-exile of a few wealthy political families, as well as American sympathizers among church and human rights activists. Largely as a result of their lobbying, the Asian and Pacific Affairs Subcommittee of the House Foreign Affairs Committee recently voted to cut a token $5 million from our security assistance request as a signal to Marcos to end martial law. The full Committee upheld the cut.[8]

CHAPTER 12

"It's Not All Greek to Me"
Bringing the Fight to the Homeland

Published photographs of Steven Elias Psinakis show him looking fierce and unsmiling, with a bearded Ayatollah Khomeini–like face and piercing eyes. Apart from Manglapus, Psinakis was the most frequently pictured member of the U.S.-based opposition in both Philippine and American media throughout the martial law years. One early photo shows him "exhausted, wearing rumpled but stylish traveling clothes," standing in a San Francisco federal court on July 6, 1987, charged with conspiracy and interstate transportation of explosive materials. He had landed at the San Francisco International Airport after a flight from Manila and was arrested upon arrival. Robert Lopez, a brother-in-law who came to the airport to meet him, was astounded: "It's very strange because Steve has come in and out of the country without any problems over the past year."[1]

At the arraignment, he pleaded not guilty and was returned to jail pending a bail hearing. He faced a sentence of up to fifteen years in prison and $20,000 in fines. He hadn't "the slightest clue why they would move against me on a case this old," he was quoted as saying in the *San Francisco Examiner*.[2] The case was indeed five years old, but the indictment had been unsealed in secret only in December 1986, days before the statute of limitations would have run out. In 1981, said the indictment, bomb paraphernalia had been found in some garbage bags at his San Francisco home. In an affidavit, San Francisco FBI special agent Larry D. Terbush said that he "recovered approximately 600 feet of detonating cord with the explosive removed . . . that would weigh approximately ten pounds and could be used to manufacture explosive bombing devices."[3]

Questions arose as soon as the indictment was unsealed. Why the five-year delay? And why at the very moment when a new democratic government was now in place? Strangest of all, four other people were originally charged in 1981, but only two had emerged as the main suspects. One was Psinakis; the other was a close associate, Charles Avila. To arrive at some answers, it is necessary to go back to the years before martial law was declared and Psinakis became involved with the U.S. exile groups.

Born in Athens, Greece, in 1931, Psinakis arrived in the United States at the age of eighteen, having been awarded a college scholarship to study engineering. He graduated from the University of Pittsburgh in 1955 with a bachelor's degree in mechanical engineering. Ten years later, he obtained U.S. citizenship. After ten years as an engineer in the United States, he worked in the Philippines for the next ten years as an operations manager for Meralco, an electric power company that served Metro Manila and was owned by Eugenio Lopez Sr. In 1969 he married Eugenio's daughter Priscilla "Presy" Lopez, and they moved to Greece. While they were in Greece, Marcos declared martial law and imprisoned Eugenio "Geny" Lopez Jr. He then took over the Lopez business properties, which in addition to Meralco included the *Manila Chronicle*, the country's second-largest newspaper, six TV and twenty-one radio stations, and all the other assets of Benpres, the holding company. Eugenio agreed to give them up in return for Geny's release. Moreover, as long as Eugenio was in San Francisco, he agreed not to speak publicly against the martial law regime.

In November 1974, with no prospect of his release, Geny decided to go on a hunger fast to draw attention to the plight of all political prisoners like himself. In a letter that he managed to secretly pass to his parents, he wrote in part: "By this act, I hope to end the humiliation and punishment that you have undergone for the past two years. Also, I hope to restore some of the dignity that rightfully belongs to any man and which you have been deprived of. You have demeaned yourself, you have been embarrassed, you have suffered enough."[4] When Marcos promised to release political prisoners, Geny and another cellmate, former president Sergio Osmena's son Sergio III, broke their forty-day hunger fast. Marcos also broke his promise.

On December 31, 1974, Eugenio Sr. reached his limit. He issued a statement to the press describing in detail how Marcos had extorted money from him for two years. "I have been blackmailed into silence, into giving up millions of dollars in my company assets. Enough is enough. I refuse to be blackmailed further. The Marcos and Romualdez families have bled me dry . . . No sooner do I comply with one of their demands th[a]n they come up with another . . . I, Eugenio Lopez, Sr. an old man, now appeal to public opinion. I have no other source to help me regain my son."[5] On July 6, 1975, Eugenio succumbed to terminal cancer. Psinakis related that "just three days before he died, he issued a last appeal. He pleaded with Marcos to send his son 'under guard' to the hospital for a final farewell. The appeal was denied."[6]

Psinakis was granted a visit to his brother-in-law Geny during his hunger fast. Geny urged Psinakis to do what he could to bring attention to their fast and to the state of the country under martial law. Once back in the United States, Psinakis was a driven man. His brother-in-law's life hung in the balance. He had to move fast. Having become a U.S. citizen, he would appeal first to the U.S. Congress. He soon discovered that lobbying for Geny's release was an expensive undertaking. "We sent a two-page telegram to every member of the U.S. Congress and important people in the media and the administration, and for that one cable alone, the cost was $5,000. I did not realize then that there's a service where you can send the same message to all members of Congress for around $400."[7]

And thus began his personal crusade to bring down the regime. In his 1981 book *Two Terrorists Meet*, Psinakis narrated every encounter with Marcos's agents and emissaries, as well as with the local U.S. officials who ignored his complaints of being harassed by Marcos agents. There were several threats on his life, he claimed, that the police politely told him they could not do anything about. The FBI, he said, had for all intents and purposes taken Marcos's side. The agency closed each case, saying that there were not enough leads to follow up. Telephone bills were running $5,000 to $6,000 a month. In the beginning, it was a one-man crusade—but a two-person campaign with Presy. After he joined the MFP in 1975, they could call on the resources of its nationwide network of chapters and members.

A large part of their information campaign was the distribution of news clippings and reports to key members of Congress describing the abuses of martial law. They targeted key decision makers on committees authorizing military and economic foreign aid to the Philippines. The reports came from well-known human rights organizations and from American private investigative missions to the Philippines. Over the years, these included "Report of an Amnesty International Mission to the Republic of the Philippines" (November 22–December 5, 1975) from Amnesty International, "Report of a Fact-Finding Mission to the Philippines" (November 28–December 17, 1983) from the Clearinghouse on Science and Human Rights of the American Association for the Advancement of Science, "The Philippines: A Country in Crisis" (December 1983) from the Lawyers Committee for International Human Rights, and "The Decline of Democracy in the Philippines" (1977) from the Geneva-based International Commission of Jurists. Most telling of all were reports from Philippines-based groups such as the Association of Major Religious Superiors of the Philippines. The reports were consistent in their documentation of tortures, killings (ironically known as "salvagings") by security forces during detention, arbitrary arrests, and searches. The Philippine government would insist that these practices were not official policy, but their widespread use, especially in remote areas, led to the firm conclusion that they were either permitted or willfully disregarded.

Drawing on these sources, Psinakis compiled a two-volume report, "The Philippines under Martial Law," in 1976 and delivered it to incoming officials of President Carter's administration, officials in the State and Justice Departments, and congressional leaders from both parties. It should be noted that the exile opposition struggled through three U.S. administrations—Presidents Gerald Ford (1973–77), Carter (1977–81), and Ronald Reagan (1981–89). The changing cast of policy makers, who might not have been familiar with the Philippine situation, required an ongoing supply of old and new reports. Psinakis was instrumental in bringing the defection and testimony of Marcos's propaganda chief, Primitivo Mijares, to the attention of Congress.

Psinakis operated from an advantageous position: He was an American citizen, unlike many of the exile leaders. Legislators listened because he was a voting constituent. His repeated contacts with a number of members of Congress put them on a first-name basis in official communications. From his opinion column "It's Not All Greek to Me" in the weekly San Francisco–based Filipino newspaper *Philippine News*, he taunted and countered announcements and news reports from Manila. With no close relatives in the Philippines whose safety had to be guarded, he pulled no punches.

Critics of Psinakis and the MFP, from their leftist allies to the Philippine government, branded them as "elite" oppositionists, a class of disenfranchised capitalists seeking nothing more than the return of their wealth and status. They alluded to Manglapus's and Psinakis's family ties—the former's wife, Pacita, and Eugenio "Geny" Lopez Jr.'s wife, Chita, are sisters.

On October 1, 1977, Psinakis engineered the escape of Geny Lopez and Serge Osmena III from a maximum-security military prison at Fort

Bonifacio in suburban Manila. Two and a half years in the planning, their adventure involved slipping out of a cell window, stuffing dummies into their beds, cutting through barbed wire, crawling across grassy ground at night, boarding a twin-engine Cessna six-seater with an American fighter pilot at the controls, making a dash to Hong Kong, using borrowed U.S. passports, and skirting immigration control in Tokyo. It took all of thirty-three hours. Upon landing in Los Angeles, Psinakis placed hurried calls to State Department contacts (nurtured by the MFP through years of lobbying). Temporary entry was authorized for Geny and Serge while their asylum requests were processed.[8]

The MFP's decision in 1979 to employ "force" in achieving its goals gave Psinakis the impetus to take his crusade a step further. He and other MFP associates linked up with the non-left oppositionists in the Philippines who became known as the LAF and A6LM. Right after the bombing incidents in Manila, the Philippine government filed charges against Aquino, Manglapus, and Psinakis, demanding that the U.S. government act on these "terrorists." Defense Secretary Enrile said that the United States could no longer "ignore the fact some of its own nationals are getting involved, using U.S.-made explosive materials."[9] There were press references to specific U.S. laws that might provide a basis for action against the MFP, including the Neutrality Act, the Arms Export Control Act, and the Foreign Agents Registration Act.

At Psinakis's meeting with Mrs. Marcos in New York on December 19, 1980, she informed him that she had met earlier with President-Elect Reagan and Vice President–Elect George Bush. According to Psinakis, she said that both leaders had committed to support the regime and to begin investigating Marcos's opponents in the United States. In June 1981, during a visit to Manila, Secretary of State Alexander Haig handed Marcos a letter from Reagan saying that the U.S. government was "following up with the FBI . . . the prosecution of terrorists operating in the Philippines and based in the United States." "She sounded confident that the Reagan administration will go after us, especially you," Aquino told Psinakis, recounting his own meeting with Mrs. Marcos on December 16 in New York. "They have evidence, she says, on your activities."[10] Sure enough, beginning in early 1981, the FBI had begun its surveillance of top MFP leaders. Agents visited Aquino, Manglapus, Psinakis, Gillego, Daza, and Alvarez at their homes.

Another MFP member was on their list—a physician in Missouri named Arturo Taca Jr. The FBI alleged, from listening in on telephone conversations, that he was a close accomplice of Psinakis. Taca, a urologist trained in the Philippines, had settled in Missouri after his arrival in the United States in 1973. He worked at several hospitals in St. Louis while maintaining a private practice in nearby Venice, Illinois. The MFP chapter that he led there had the largest number of Filipino physician members, five of them officers. His unpublished 131-page memoir of their chapter's history describes quarrelsome relations with the doctors belonging to the Association of Philippine Practicing Physicians in America (APPA). In 1972, out of 8,846 Filipino physicians in the United States, Taca estimated that only 10 percent were APPA members. The APPA, he concluded, was a conservative group of pro-Marcos physicians whose wives loved to party and flaunt their expensive attire at their annual conventions.[11] He had an agenda in joining APPA—to gain a leadership position and steer the association toward MFP goals. He was rebuffed at every turn.

Taca's feelings of antipathy toward his colleagues deepened when Aquino was not invited to speak at the association's convention in Boston in 1982. And at the Chicago convention in 1983, the APPA leadership refused requests by members to observe a minute of silence in memory of the slain Aquino. "Even the priest who delivered the invocation apparently had been cowed," he wrote. "The leadership even had the temerity of attempting to cut short the singing of the patriotic song 'Bayan Ko' by the Detroit doctors' group. What was thoroughly nauseating was the sight of the representative of the hated Marcos government being accorded the most honored guest status. Obviously the moral bearings of the leadership of the APPA had been lost."[12] Aquino had stood as a sponsor or "Ninong" at Taca's wedding, and he was also the baptismal godfather to one of Taca's children. Among Filipinos, such cultural ties bind beyond the religious associations. It was therefore no surprise that Taca was more than willing to work with Psinakis when his "Ninong" asked him to.

The FBI claimed that Taca had supplied the explosive materials, which were shipped by Greyhound bus from St. Louis to Psinakis's residence. In February 1982, two agents came to interview Taca at his home. They questioned him, fishing for information about his contacts with Psinakis and others from the MFP, any trips he had taken to Arizona and California, any knowledge he might have about detonation cords, the LAF, and the A6LM. He denied everything. Before leaving, they handed him a subpoena to appear before a federal grand jury in San Francisco on March 8, 1982. At that appearance, Taca refused to testify against Psinakis in exchange for immunity. In an interview with the *San Francisco Examiner*, "he vowed to go to jail rather than testify. But he also contended that there was absolutely nothing wrong with trying to bring down Marcos by any means necessary."[13]

Years later, Taca's son Coco, remembering his father's death in 1997, remarked that his father's "political reputation wasn't as sexy [as that of the other defendants]. Everyone thought my dad would rat. Rumors in Manila papers had written bad things about him and his perceived change of heart. Well, despite the possibility of losing everything, his family, flourishing medical practice, a comfortable life, my dad did not talk."[14] Taca was identified as an accomplice but was acquitted.

Near midnight on December 17, 1981, a convoy of cars glided into the street in southwest San Francisco where Psinakis's Spanish-style home was located. About a score of men from the FBI and the San Francisco police surrounded the house. They were armed with a search warrant authorizing them to look for "certain destructive materials." Psinakis, Presy, and their children were herded into the kitchen and told to stay there while the search party rummaged through the rooms. Charles Avila, who happened to be visiting that night, was also ordered to stay in the kitchen throughout the search. They found nothing. They had been made to believe that the bomb-making paraphernalia the FBI had recovered days earlier in garbage bags from Psinakis's residence would lead to more incriminating materials inside the house. At a press conference later, Psinakis suggested that "a Marcos agent" could have planted the alleged bomb-making materials in his garbage.

After three and a half hours, the searchers left. They took the contents of Avila's briefcase and shoulder bag—an unloaded pistol, documents, pictures of activists in the Philippines. Most troubling of all to Psinakis, they went through the files and correspondence in his upstairs study, some of which contained names of his contacts in the Philippines. "Three weeks after the raid I learned from my intelligence sources in the Philippines that copies of the documents seized or photographed were on the desk of General Fabian Ver in Manila. A week later I learned that more than 20 people had been arrested in Manila for interrogation. Most of them were tortured and two disappeared and were presumed salvaged," he said.[15]

On September 6, 1980, an explosion rocked a room in the YMCA Hostel on Concepcion Street in Manila. A thirty-five-year-old Filipino naturalized American, Victor Burns Lovely Jr., lost his right arm and left eye and suffered damaged hearing in one ear. When he regained consciousness after ten days in a hospital, he was under heavy guard. Five weeks later, he signed a twelve-page confession at the Armed Forces of the Philippines Medical Center. The statement was released November 1 to the Manila press together with photos showing Lovely heavily bandaged, signing a paper. His confession contained the following admissions:

- He had come to Manila the month before from Los Angeles, California, where he had managed a Filipino food store supplying nine navy commissaries in the United States.
- He was sent to plant bombs in hotels, schools, government buildings, and government vehicles, "in that order."
- Former senator Jovito Salonga was to be his contact in supplying the bomb materials, which were delivered by a lawyer named Renato "Nits" Tanada in a Puma bag at a meeting at Salonga's house.
- After each bomb was placed, he would call the Associated Press and United Press International and leave a message: "This is the April 6th Movement. We have planted a bomb on [targets], and we would like to inform you that we don't want people to get hurt. The bomb will explode in [X] minutes."
- The bombing was part of a "destabilization" plan by "trained urban guerrillas" to topple the Marcos regime.
- He and four other U.S.-based people spent four days in an Arizona desert training in "urban guerrilla warfare, explosives and demolition, small arms and Armalites."
- The Movement for a Free Philippines was the principal planner, organizer, and financier of the plan.
- The principal "operations director" was Steve Psinakis. Aquino was also behind the plan. All the top MFP officers were involved, from Manglapus to Gillego, Alvarez, and Daza.
- When all the Light-A-Fire bombers were captured together, it was decided to split up the guerrillas into three-men cell teams, with each cell having no knowledge of the members of the other cells.
- The destabilization plan must succeed before the 1980 U.S. presidential elections, because if Reagan were to win, he would give the Philippines more aid. If Carter won, he would restrict aid on account of the Marcoses' human rights record.

In all, Lovely identified more than twenty people belonging to all the U.S.-based opposition groups plus the MFP—the FFP, the KDP, and the Ninoy Aquino Movement.

Years later, in an affidavit submitted in 1988 at the trial in San Francisco of Psinakis, Lovely said: "the confession was prepared by my interrogators and . . . was not shown to me until it was presented for immediate signature; . . . I was later made to appear on television, purportedly in spontaneous live interviews, when in fact, the interviews were staged, rehearsed and pre-recorded by my captors."[16] But before then, Lovely had to endure a bizarre judicial process to force him to testify in an American court. While waiting for his trial to proceed in Manila, he languished for a year in a military prison. On September 28, 1981, he was secretly flown to the United States to testify before a federal grand jury, although there was no extradition treaty between the two countries. The main target of the grand jury probe was Psinakis. U.S. prosecutors finally had a live witness, against not only him but also other MFP members.

But when Lovely appeared before the U.S. District Court on February 9, 1982, he invoked the Fifth Amendment against self-incrimination and refused to testify even after receiving a grant of immunity. He was immediately hit with a contempt of court charge and sent to prison. Suffering from claustrophobia that he said became unbearable (he feared that he "would either become deranged or die"), he agreed to testify, implicating Psinakis, Aquino, Manglapus, Avila, and Daza.[17] With their investigation complete by early 1982, U.S. prosecutors were ready to indict, but they suddenly decided not to proceed. According to the government, "indictments have been prepared against leaders of the organization and will be presented before the grand jury at a later date. This matter has been held in abeyance because of the Aquino assassination [in August 1983]."[18] Lawyers for Psinakis said that "those indictments were, however never presented to the grand jury. Instead a second grand jury was convened in March of 1985. The testimony of Lovely and apparently, other evidence against Senator Aquino and other Filipino opposition leaders, was not presented to that grand jury. Instead, as it appeared, evidence against Mr. Psinakis was carefully selected from among the evidence contained in 1981 which had been presented to the prior grand jury. An indictment was returned on December 2, 1986, nearly five years to the day after the occurrence of the events alleged in the indictment."[19]

So when Psinakis stepped on American soil that July day in 1987, unbeknownst to him, a five-year-old indictment against him was unsealed. The new government in Manila reacted strongly in surprise. Manglapus, who had been appointed as foreign secretary by President Corazon Aquino, protested in a letter to Secretary of State George P. Shultz, "Our people are trying to forgive and forget the [U.S. government's] support of the ruthless Marcos dictatorship until its collapse in February 1986. Prosecuting Psinakis would surely open wounds."[20]

Notes surfaced from the prosecution side during the hearings hinting that the U.S. State Department had been worried as early as 1986 that the trial would implicate people already holding important positions in the Aquino government, namely Manglapus himself, Gillego, Daza, and Alvarez. By August 1986, Alvarez was minister of agrarian reform; Gillego was the executive director of the Philippine Commission on Good Government, working to locate the hidden holdings of Marcos and his wife; Daza was a member of that commission. By 1988, Daza and Gillego had been elected as congressional representatives, and Alvarez was a senator.[21] Psinakis's defense successfully argued that the case was politically motivated. In other words, political decisions were made not to prosecute certain people and to focus only on Psinakis.

The U.S. prosecution team was not happy with his acquittal. Granted that he and his associates were working for a good cause, said the assistant U.S. attorney, "anyone who knowingly violates the law for whatever moral reason ought to have the integrity to admit it and suffer the consequences. That's what Psinakis is in court for. If the charges are true, then he was shipping explosives on Greyhound buses where passengers were located. Where do you draw the line? It can't be the case where the jurors have to decide if they agree on a defendant's moral principles or not. Ferdinand Marcos was perhaps a very evil guy to have running the Philippines, but we can't allow that to dictate how we enforce the laws of this country."[22]

Not so, said Psinakis's lawyers. They submitted a memorandum charging that at the time the U.S. government, at the request of Marcos, was vigorously pursuing his opponents in the United States, it was ignoring the actions of similar groups in the country whom it considered its allies. They documented U.S. support of the U.S.-based Iranian dissidents against the American-supported shah, the "contras" against the Nicaraguan leftist Sandinistas, the Cuban exiles against the Communist Castro, and the Afghan guerrillas against the Soviet occupation of Afghanistan. In each case, they charged, mercenaries were training on U.S. soil and shipping explosives. When Congress found out, it pushed for investigations, but the administration scuttled any moves to stop its assistance. "It is now clear that private groups supporting the overthrow of governments in Central America have engaged with the complicity of the U.S. government, in massive violations of the very laws under which Mr. Psinakis is charged in this case."[23]

CHAPTER 13

A Man for Many Seasons

The Leader Who Led the Movement

The four-page FBI file on Manglapus, dated March 6, 1981, lists his physical attributes: "Sex: male; Nationality: Filipino; Date of birth: October 20, 1918; Height: approximately five feet, seven inches; Weight: approximately 140 pounds; Hair: black; Eyes: brown; Race: white; Residence: 6616 Melrose Drive, McLean, Virginia." No one looking at him would see a white male; he was evidently and truly a brown Asian. A *New York Times* correspondent saw a "short, compact man." In a newspaper photo of his arrival in Manila in 1986, right after the deposed Marcos had fled the country, the returning sixty-eight-year-old exile, welcomed as a hero, sported an inky black crew cut, looking for all the world like an eighteen-year-old student.

There is another photo of him that a Jesuit priest who has lived in the Philippines close to fifty years, Fr. James Reuter, remembers seeing posted on the bulletin board of the Jesuits' Xavier House dormitory in Manila. It shows Manglapus "in prison—dark, crew cut, very thin, and with the unmistakable prisoner's look."[1] Having been arrested by the dreaded Japanese military police corps, the Kempeitai, for his work as a radio broadcaster for General Douglas MacArthur's Press Relations Office, he was dragged from one prison to another—fifty-seven days at Fort Santiago, six months at Old Bilibid, sixteen months in Muntinlupa. His Japanese guards tortured him and his fellow prisoners for weeks with blows, bats, slaps, and "withering torrents of 'Tagarrog' obscenities."[2] The Japanese had wanted them to reveal the names of their broadcast colleagues.

On August 25, 1944, he and more than a hundred prisoners escaped from Muntinlupa, groping their way out during a moonless night. He resumed his Voice of Freedom radio broadcasts and then joined the Hunters guerrilla unit attached to the U.S. 11th Airborne Division. Accredited as a war correspondent with General MacArthur's command, he witnessed the formal surrender of Japan. When Japan signed the surrender papers aboard the battleship USS *Missouri* in Tokyo Bay on September 2, 1945, he might have been the youngest non-American on board. From the Yokohama hotel where the war correspondents attending the event were staying, they had to cross a small bridge to the general's hotel to see him. The bridge was guarded by two demobilized Japanese soldiers, unarmed save for short ceremonial swords. "Each time we passed by, the guards would bow to us with great respect, we liked to think. I must have crossed that bridge 70 times a day, just to get two Japanese soldiers to bow to me for a change," Manglapus wrote in a short memoir of his prisoner experience. Said Fr. Reuter: "It is no small thing to break out of a Japanese military prison. It is harder to do than to break out of a Marcos prison during martial law."[3]

In truth, Manglapus was an involuntary detainee in the United States as a self-exile—thirteen years, five months, and seven days by his count, beginning in 1972, when by sheer luck he found himself in America the day before martial law clamped down on the Philippines. Officially, at least, four court charges had been filed against him during his exile years, including subversion, rebellion, and plotting to kill Marcos and his wife. If he had returned, there is no doubt that he would have been hauled off to jail as soon as he stepped out of the plane. He had left behind an outstanding career that was cut short. Those who speculated about what he might have accomplished in his country without Marcos referred to his impressive record as a legislator and public servant. They started with his schooling—he had graduated *summa cum laude* from the Jesuit university Ateneo de Manila, earning a Bachelor of Arts degree; he had then studied law at the same university, at the University of Santo Tomas in Manila, and at Georgetown University in Washington, D.C. His oratorical skills had been honed in various high school and college contests. He took the gold medal at a College Editors Guild debate in 1938, where he defended, ironically, the topic "Dictatorship Is the Best Form of Government for the Philippines." He composed the Ateneo's official song, "Fly High Blue Eagle," and sang at the university's basketball games.

When Manglapus was named secretary of foreign affairs in 1957, he was, at thirty-five, the youngest ever to occupy that position. Previously, as undersecretary, he had initiated the Foreign Service Officers examinations over the violent objections of politicians who saw in these examinations a diminution of political patronage. He resigned that post for his first venture into political life. He lost in his first run for the Senate in 1955, then lost again in 1959. He won on his third try, in 1961, garnering the highest number of votes. It was during his six years in the Senate that he made his mark as an innovative legislator. As co-author of the Revised Barrio Charter and the Decentralization Bill of 1964, he promoted greater participation of local communities in national life. To workers and employees, this legislation offered a "people's capitalism," a wider distribution of productive property. He championed cooperatives and inspired and engineered the acquisition of government textile mills by their workers. He also sponsored the revolutionary Land Reform Code.

Unhappy with the two parties that dominated the electoral process, Manglapus and several senators formed a new party, the Progressive Party of the Philippines. It chose him to run for president in 1965 against two powerful opponents—the incumbent, Diosdado Macapagal, and the president of the Senate, Ferdinand Marcos. Lacking an extensive political machinery, however, such as a sufficient number of poll watchers, the party lost, and with it went the viability of a third party. The humbling experience led to the founding of his Christian Social Movement in 1968.

In 1970, Manglapus was elected a delegate to the Constitutional Convention, representing the First District of Rizal, the largest electoral district. He received the highest number of votes. He and a number of delegates—Alvarez and Gillego among them—formed a "Progressive Bloc," trying to thwart Marcos's efforts to draft a new constitution that would allow him a third term. That would be their final campaign on home grounds before their extended exile.

They switched from crafting a new Philippine constitution to demonizing a man and a regime—this in essence was their new cause in the United States. They believed that in order to restore democracy, the dictatorship must be dismantled first. They devoted every waking hour to this pursuit, marshaling all the resources at their disposal—speeches, lobbying, media relations, event planning, and opinion pieces in American publications— and ultimately linking up with moderate allies back home who had resorted to violence. In stark terms, they were encouraging Filipino immigrants to be disloyal to the Philippine government. It would take a significant amount of rationalizing to convince them that their lobbying against military aid and the U.S. bases did not mean that they were helping the Communists win. The Filipino moderates in the United States argued that the Philippine army needed the arms to fight back against the Communists.

The MFP chapters were reporting that the bombings in Manila were discouraging donations, would-be recruits, and even their own members. "Although the bombings provided a resounding message to the regime, their results were not as impressive," said David Pacis, a political scientist who studied the organization.

> The bolder attempts signaled disappointment with the regime and show-cased the exiles' abilities to engage in formidable strategies. Likewise the impression of chaos the terrorists created caused a drop in business confidence. At the same time, however, the regime's retaliation and American involvement made the costs of exile opposition higher. It is also important to point out that although the exiles adopted radical programs often associated with the ultra-left—in the Philippines, the NPA and the MNLF—there was no change in ideology. The MFP remained moderate in character seeking to use a radical tool for a different purpose. Unlike the violence espoused by leftist organizations, the urban bombings were intended not to overthrow by revolution, but to urge Marcos, at the very least, to call for free and fair elections.
>
> What did the ventures into urban guerrilla warfare contribute to the transition to democracy? Many of the exiles claimed that such efforts were necessary and forced Marcos to initiate moves toward normalization. To others, the terrorism was a waste of resources. Not only did it detract money and energy from normal activities, but the ensuing harassment by Marcos loyalists and U.S. agencies also spread an aura of fear among the exiles to the point of paralysis.[4]

As head of the main exile opposition group, Manglapus had to deal with the challenges of a new leadership role. As a seasoned politician back home, he possessed the skills to respond to his constituents, both local and national. But in the United States, the tactics needed to win over Congress and the Filipino residents required a different set of skills. A learning curve had to be scaled.

Keeping the organization intact in the face of internal and external conflicts was labor-intensive. Pacis noted that commands from exile leaders were rarely binding. Instead, compliance with their rule was a matter of voluntary consent on the part of members. The MFP adherents of the LAF and A6LM members knew that Manglapus would not officially endorse their activity. So they simply went around him. Psinakis and Alvarez met with Mrs. Marcos in New York, aware that Manglapus would not approve of it if they told him in advance.

Perhaps what made the MFP such a successful lobbying force could be attributed to the abilities of the man himself. A gifted orator, writer, and scholar, Manglapus was ideally suited to the task at hand. Because an exile opposition must work with the home opposition, it was essential that he be accepted as a worthy exile leader by the home front. Manglapus had forged that relationship during his Senate days, his campaigns for that office, and his third-party pursuit of the presidency in 1965.

It would have been difficult to find somebody to replace him. The MFP's two-year presidential term was amended to extend his tenure three times. Manglapus recognized what he brought to the job. On the eve of the 1979 MFP elections to choose a new leader, he wrote a chapter chairman to request his support: "It is inevitable that the leader and the militant, ideological, or revolutionary movement that he leads get identified together in the public mind. I do not mean to compare ours with the giant movements which, in spite of ideological orientation in historic terms, got to be known as Maoism, Castroism, Stalinism, Leninism, or Hitlerism. But every contemporary movement, of whatever size, has its leader with which it eventually gets identified and will be the target of attacks from both (left and right) extremes."[5]

During the first years of martial law, domestic political opposition had been virtually silenced. Those who were able to raise their voices in protest had made their peace with the administration. The population was lulled into believing that the suspension of civil liberties would be temporary and was willing to accept it in exchange for order and peace. It was during this period that the exile opposition was seen as the only voice against the regime. Said Hilarion Henares, a *Philippine Daily Inquirer* columnist, "When most of our leaders were incarcerated in military camps, when there was no voice of protest over the land, Raul Manglapus spoke eloquently and passionately on our behalf."[6]

"In our years of exile, we presumptuously compared our appeals in Washington to those of Rizal in Madrid, drawing parallels for our success, failures, internal dissension and methods of survival with those of the [old exiles]," Manglapus recalled in 1987, in a lecture delivered after his return.[7] He was referring to Jose Rizal, the national hero who was exiled to Spain during its colonial rule of the Philippines. It was a romantic comparison that enticed younger, idealistic new immigrants to join the MFP.

This was perhaps one motive that inspired Manglapus to compose a musical play. While at Cornell University in New York in 1974 as a research associate with its Southeast Asia Program, he could easily have produced yet another of the dense political science treatises that policy think tanks churned out regularly but that no one ever read. Instead, said Manglapus, "I wanted to reach a wider audience, so I decided to do something I had had in mind for many years. That is to express some of my views in the form of a musical comedy. The head of the program seemed a bit surprised I must admit when I told him what I planned to do, but he told me to go ahead."[8] The result was a musical history, expressed in lyrics, of how America, in pursuit of its "Manifest Destiny," decided to annex the Philippines as its first colony. "The play is not about the present martial law situation in the islands, and yet, in a way it is," wrote Art Zich in a letter to a colleague at the U.S. magazine *Newsweek* who reviewed plays and other cultural events. "It is 'about' the U.S. interruption in what might have been a natural historical evolution (the great Filipino intellectual freedom fighter, Mabini, like Ho Chi Minh, quoted Jefferson in his Declaration). By extension, it is 'about' what the U.S. continues to do, in lieu of policy, in Southeast Asia—to allow drift, and the interests of the commerce boys to take the place of what a lot of us think the U.S. still stands for."[9]

Manifest Destiny: An Evening of Yankee Panky had its premiere in Honolulu on July 5 and 7, 1974. It was performed for two nights at the Cathedral of St. John the Divine in Manhattan in September 1988. At Manila's Rizal Theater, it played for three nights in May 1988. The cast of characters includes everyone who figured prominently in the annexation—from Teddy Roosevelt to Commodore Dewey, from Senator Beveridge to President William McKinley: "they are all there . . . , as if it were an instant playback—the hypocrisy, the deceit, the betrayal, the vicious greed, the love-hate that characterize Philippine American relations today as we prepare for the Bases Treaty negotiations," wrote Henares.[10]

Manglapus's talent as a playwright was complemented by his jazz skills. He was known to have "jammed" with Norodom Sihanouk, the former monarch of Cambodia; with King Aduldet Phumiphol of Thailand; and with the American jazz great Duke Ellington. "Of course, with the Duke at the piano, I moved over to the drums."[11]

The MFP was never under the illusion that exile activity alone would bring down the dictatorship. There were other anti-Marcos forces with outside bases or outside help and their own agendas to overpower Marcos and take over the country. The MFP served as the overseas arm of the nonviolent democratic opposition at home advocating a multiparty constitutional government. The Communists sought central authoritarian rule via the armed struggle of the New People's Army (NPA). It had an exile office in Holland and a leader, Jose Maria Sison, drawing funds from European sources. The Moro National Liberation Movement (MNLF) in Mindanao campaigned for autonomy. Its leader, Nur Misuari, won the patronage of Libyan strongman Muammar Gaddafi, who, in the name of Muslim brotherhood, supplied arms.

Facing a common enemy, they worked together on occasions when they deemed that it served their distinct agendas. But Manglapus was clear about where he drew the line: "We stand in admiration of the driving commitment of the NPA to fight [the] dictatorship. But we can never accept the NPA's version of a dictatorship of the proletariat. As for the MNLF, we have more than once announced publicly that, pursuant to a 1978 MFP Convention resolution, we have established contact with its leaders. We sympathize with the historic aspirations for justice and autonomy of our brother and sister Muslim Filipinos whom [Marcos] drove to rebellion with [his] duplicity. They have assured us they do not seek secession."[12]

Upon Marcos's downfall, the new government quickly began to reestablish the democratic institutions he had dismantled. At elections for a new Congress, Manglapus won a seat, proving that even after his long absence, the electorate remembered his impressive Senate accomplishments before the martial law years. It also disproved the contention that he had become irrelevant during the lengthy period when he was removed from the home struggle. In essence, they recognized and appreciated his work as an exile in helping to restore democracy.

In 1987, President Corazon Aquino named him foreign secretary and assigned him to negotiate the next bases agreement with the United States. He would be sitting across the table from American negotiators with the same mindset as those he had faced in Washington, D.C., during his exile years, namely, that both countries needed the bases. That premise was not negotiable. The talks would merely deal with the money—how much and for how long.

The first agreement, in 1947, had given the Americans a ninety-nine-year lease to sixteen bases, including the Subic Bay Naval Base and Clark Air Base. The U.S. had already spent $100 million in building their infrastructures. Over the years, through the sheer size of their expansions, they had come to dwarf all the other U.S. bases in the Pacific. In land area, Clark was the fourth-largest air base in the world. Its runway stretched two miles, and its parking area could hold two hundred aircraft. A forty-three-mile pipeline connected it with Subic's naval supply depot, which could store 110 million gallons of petroleum, oil, and lubricants. Subic occupied eighteen square miles of land and forty square miles of deep harbor water. Its three wharves and three floating dry docks could service aircraft carriers, destroyers, submarines, and guided missile cruisers. One report said that at least since the early 1960s, nuclear-powered ships had docked at Subic, and planes with nuclear weapons had landed at Clark.[13] "The Philippines represent our farthest forward outpost, our last dam, our front trenches, if you will," declared Admiral John S. McCain Jr. during hearings on May 18, 1976, before the House Committee on International Relations. "If we were to lose the Philippines, our next fallback position would be Guam, the trust territories, then Honolulu, and then the West Coast."[14]

When the 1947 lease was signed, the Philippines was in the position of having to take what it could get. Still struggling out of the ruins of World War II, heavily dependent on aid from the United States to recover, and fearing the loss of American protection, it readily accepted the bases, as well as U.S. jurisdiction over Filipinos working inside them. The United States' arrogance over its dominant position was illustrated at a 1956 meeting to revise the agreement. "The chief U.S. negotiator shoved a paper across the table to his counterpart, Emmanuel Pelaez, saying, 'Here is your position.' Pelaez, then a senator and later vice president, stalked out, stalling the talks for two years."[15]

Three decades later, with the original agreement set to expire in 1991, the political atmosphere surrounding the bases had undergone a profound transformation. A national debate was sweeping the country. Whose interests did the bases serve? American or Philippine? What were those interests? The last negotiations in 1979, when Marcos was still in power, had secured a $500 million aid package over the next five years. "Our dignity and sovereignty can no longer be bought," declared vocal nationalists. The bases perpetuated dependency, bred prostitution and crime in the Olongapo and Angeles towns surrounding them, and exploited the Filipino workers. The country, they added, was ostracized by its Southeast Asian neighbors for harboring these vestiges of colonial rule. Ironically, these neighbors wanted the bases to stay, to provide the region a nuclear security "umbrella" in the Cold War, as long as they were in the Philippines, and not on their own soil, infringing on their sovereignties. Manglapus had always believed that Marcos had used the Americans and their bases to stay in power for as long as he did. He wrote:

> The powerful shadow of America remains cast over our land. The Americans solved their problem by crawling away from the British shadow,

thus speeding their growth. But the long fixed shadow of Subic and Clark stretches over the land and mind of the Filipino.

There is a certain amount of thinking that if all goes wrong, we can go running to Uncle Sam to fix it and this is something that is not useful.[16]

"We must first slay the American father image and cut him down to brotherly size" was one memorable quote from him during the bases negotiations that he presided over.[17]

Riding the nationalist wave, in 1991 the Philippine Senate ultimately rejected the treaty to extend the bases agreement. A bitter lesson had been learned, fallout from the nation's agony during martial law—never again would it allow anyone, however powerful, to coddle a brutal pet dictator for the sake of its foreign interests. At the turnover ceremonies on November 24 of that year, the American flag was lowered at the Subic Bay Naval Base for the final time. (Clark Air Base had closed earlier, damaged beyond repair by the volcanic eruption of nearby Mt. Pinatubo.)[18]

"The United States saved Filipinos the trouble of having to shed more blood, and we should give credit," Manglapus said in a 1986 interview with the *New York Times*. "While I suppose we should thank them, we could also ask, what took so long?" He cautioned the U.S. not to congratulate itself too much, arguing that it could have eased out Marcos years ago. Instead, he said, "American leaders over the years had submitted to 'blackmail' in their desire to hold onto their naval and air bases."[19]

"Since then, America's 'father image' has indeed faded," the *Times* wrote in an obituary for Manglapus, who died from cancer on July 25, 1999, at the age of eighty. "Externally, Manila has begun to strengthen ties with its regional neighbors, moving away from its single-minded focus on the United States. At home, it has worked to build a more independent national identity."[20] "I think the slaying has happened," he had been quoted as saying earlier, "non-violently, diplomatically and to the satisfaction of the slayer and the slain."[21]

Epilogue

The fourteen-year agony of Marcos's rule ended with his hasty escape from Manila on February 26, 1986. The situation in the country when he left was as bad as or even worse than it had been when he took over the presidency in 1965. At his inaugural address he had spoken of a "venal government . . . a barren treasury . . . a slothful civil service . . . a demoralized armed forces." Fourteen years into his martial law presidency, the country had gone downhill. According to the Food and Nutrition Institute of the Philippines, 70 percent of the population was suffering from malnutrition, and a University of the Philippines study showed that 68 percent of all Filipino households lived below the poverty level.[1]

In the 1960s, Benigno Aquino looked at his country and saw both the good and the bad. "Here is a land in which a few are spectacularly rich while the masses remain abjectly poor," he said. "Here is a land consecrated to democracy but run by an entrenched plutocracy. Here, too, are a people whose ambitions run high, but whose fulfillment is low and mainly restricted to the self-perpetuating élite."[2] His wife, President Corazon Aquino, inherited both worlds when she took over in 1986. She served for six years, followed by three presidents (one of whom was unseated peacefully by another People Power revolt). A new president was elected in May 2010, who happens to be her son, a senator who was propelled into the presidency by the mass mourning that marked her death during the election campaign period.

Where does the Philippines now stand in the second decade of the twenty-first century, twenty-five years after the bloodless People Power transition to democracy? There are bright spots: in school enrollment and life expectancy, the country compares favorably with its closest Asian neighbors, Thailand, Indonesia, and Malaysia. It lags behind them in per capita income, however, and indicators for income distribution and poverty are dismal. More than a third of Filipinos live below the poverty level; the top 10 percent of income earners hold 31 percent of the wealth, compared to only 2.4 percent for the bottom 10 percent.[3] Benigno Aquino's 1960 landscape of mass abject poverty among the few spectacularly rich has not been altered by the revolutions. Beyond these economic indicators, an observer claimed to have identified a distinct trait in the Filipino character that explained why it had not progressed as well as its "tiger" neighbors. James Fallows, an American magazine writer, asserted in 1987 that Filipinos suffered from a "damaged culture" that had led to a failed sense of nationhood: "Filipinos pride themselves on their lifelong loyalty to family, schoolmates, compadres, members of the same tribe, residents of the same *barangay* . . . Because the boundaries of decent treatment are limited to the family or tribe, they exclude at least 90 percent of the people in the country . . . When a country with extreme geographic, tribal and social class differences, like the Philippines, has only a weak offsetting sense of national unity, its public life does become the war of every man against every man."[4] Some Filipinos describe this characterization as still valid today, calling it the "crab mentality," with people furiously clawing their way up and over each other in an attempt to get ahead.

How, then, were a culturally "damaged" people able to harness the collective will to overthrow a dictator? Indeed, a number of equally influential historians of Asia questioned the validity of culture as a primary determinant of economic and political failure. It is a simplistic sociology of development that argues that a society can be considered developed if it possesses a different set of values and norms, preferably Western. Fallows should have considered that other cultural trait of Filipinos—the ability of strong kinship, family and community ties, famously known as the "bayanihan" spirit—to overcome adversity. The four-day peaceful revolt of February 1986 was a dramatic manifestation of this spirit.

As a result, political freedom has flourished. The rebuilt institutions— the press, the legislature, the courts—are not perfect, but after a quarter of a century, they have taken root where before they had withered. Unlike other developing countries that suddenly transitioned to democracy but lacked the institutions to sustain it, the Philippines was fortunate that before martial law, it possessed the institutional scaffolding needed to re-build. Moreover, there was a unifying force or leader—Corazon Aquino and the memory of her martyred husband, who led the restoration. The euphoria that seized the population, that the downfall of one man would make everything right, heightened the expectations for a better future. It did not happen. Filipinos today are realizing that the country's underde-velopment cannot be blamed entirely on the fourteen years of martial law.

The exiles returning home in 1986 knew that they were going back to a ravaged homeland. Alfred McCoy, the historian who uncovered the Maharlika documents, tallied the horrific results of fourteen years of martial law: 3,257 extrajudicial killings, 35,000 cases of torture, 70,000 illegal jailings, and 737 unexplained disappearances between 1975 and 1985.[5] The rebuilding could now begin—through public service by Man-glapus, Gillego, Avila, Daza, Alvarez, and Osmena III. Ortigas returned to direct the Asian Institute of Management. Lopez Jr. reclaimed the com-munications companies that had been parceled out to Marcos cronies and built them up once again into the country's largest. Psinakis joined one of its units, Meralco, as a high-ranking officer. Bello was elected to the House of Representatives in 2007.[6] In grateful recognition of their overseas service, a Manila-based foundation, the Bantayog Ng Mga Bay-ani, has enshrined in a Memorial Center the names of Benigno Aquino Jr., Gillego, Gaston, Manglapus, and Taca among the 207 martyrs and heroes of the martial law period. Also remembered were the murdered labor union members of the KDP chapter in Seattle, Washington—Gene A. Viernes and Silme G. Domingo.[7] As of November 30, 2011, they were the only exile leaders to have been accorded this honor (Bantayog names are nominated each year).

Before he returned to Manila, Gillego moved into an office in the Philip-pine consulate on Fifth Avenue in Manhattan, the site of numerous anti-martial law demonstrations. As the first executive director of the newly created Philippine Commission on Good Government, he was tasked with tracking down the millions of dollars' worth of assets that Marcos and his wife had accumulated and secreted overseas. In New York City alone, the real estate included four high-rise office buildings in Manhat-tan, a shopping mall, a townhouse, and properties in suburban New York and New Jersey.

How did the victors deal with those who collaborated with the re-gime? Notorious Marcos cronies had fled the country, mindful that Filipino collaborators with the Japanese occupying forces during World War II were harshly punished (much like the French collaborators with the German Nazis). Martial law was more than one man sustaining a repressive system by himself. Hundreds, even thousands, willingly carried out his decrees. There were career economists and scientific technicians in Marcos's service who "by their international acceptance have lent credibility to his dictatorship and facilitated the prolongation of the people's agony," Manglapus charged.[8] Sadly, Filipinos have short memories. How else can one explain Imelda Marcos's return in 1992, the ultimate symbol of shameless extravagance amid abject poverty, yet permitted to run for the presidency, taking fifth place out of seven candidates? Then in 1995, her constituents elected her as a congresswoman representing a district from her hometown; she again won a seat in 2010, representing a district in the province of her dead husband. International observers shook their heads in disbelief and reflected on the absurdity of the situation.

The Philippine exiles faced some unusual hurdles in their struggle. Their efforts were challenged not only by their homeland adversaries. Their host country, the United States, was both ally—those in the legislative branch of the Congress who were sympathetic to their cause; and opponent—those in the executive branch and their like-minded partners in agencies such as the State Department, the Pentagon, and the FBI. That the exiles' struggle took so long was due partly to the narrow perspective of these policy makers, who were guided by misconceived priorities. Another factor that prolonged the Marcos regime and brought the exiles to the brink of exhaustion was the degree of its repression. It tolerated just enough dissent to defuse the buildup of a widespread rebellion. By shrewdly working the levers—when to crack down, when to ease up—Marcos kept his enemies guessing and confused. The result, it was argued, was not an absolute dictatorship.

Others suggest that hungry people have no stomach for political activism. Seven years into martial law, it was enough of a struggle for an undernourished population to put food on the table, let alone fight human rights abuses. Dissent was a luxury. But by the last years of martial law, as the regime teetered, both the homeland opposition and the exiles coordinated their tactics more closely. When their homeland forces faltered, the exiles strengthened their resolve to make up the slack. For example, although the Manila bombings did not ignite a mass uprising, they caused Marcos some worry because the bombers were not the usual Communists but rather a new breed of inspired "terrorists." Security was tightened, provoking more arbitrary detentions, which in turn aroused increased disgust toward the regime among the homeland Filipinos.

How much more could the exiles have done to accelerate the transition process? They were perfectly positioned to conduct their primary mission of lobbying, but this kind of work was tedious, the battleground kept shifting, and the principal policy makers were difficult to pin down. The exiles had to play by the ground rules of their host country's decision-making process, and such compliance was time-consuming. The apathy of the majority of immigrant Filipinos remained pervasive to the end; it lessened somewhat when Aquino was assassinated, but the enthusiasm petered out and never swelled again. The exiles mobilized in force in a strong show of protest in Washington, D.C., during the Marcos state visit in September 1982. But they were outdone by the resources of the government as well as by the pomp and panoply laid out by a friendly Reagan administration.

We can only imagine how things would have been different if the exiles and activists had been able to use the internet and smart phones—technologies supremely adapted for mobilization. It is debatable whether such modern communication tools would truly have facilitated their efforts to mobilize the Filipino immigrant communities, but there is no doubt that these tools would have significantly expedited the exchange of news between homeland and exile oppositionists. Bad news about the regime could have been spread with digital velocity to the Filipino immigrants by the exiles. But to move from being aware to actually participating was a step that took much more effort to achieve. The Marcos dictatorship was a unique historic event in its impact on Filipinos in the United States. No other unifying issue has emerged since then with comparable force. About 11 million Filipinos now live and work overseas, in scores of countries, but despite the Overseas Absentee Voting Act, implemented in 2003, a "lively virtual political community in cyberspace is not echoed in their participation in national elections," noted Professor David Camroux during a conference session examining Philippine government relations with overseas Filipinos. It may take another seismic political event to test the effectiveness of "social media" in mobilizing emigrant Filipino minds and hearts.[9]

The exile oppositionists did not have the advantage of social media as a tool for change. They had to depend on face-to-face mobilization in the manner that Canadian journalist Malcolm Gladwell describes in connection with the U.S. civil rights movement during the 1960s. The black students organized their protests "without e-mail, texting, Facebook or Twitter," wrote Gladwell, questioning the effectiveness of social networking in contemporary revolutionary activity.[10]

The MFP's leadership base, headquartered in Washington, D.C., was at the best of times a part-time band of activists. Volunteers came and went. They had day jobs to attend to. Driven by an ideal, they struggled with minuscule financial resources and minimal staff. Let us imagine again how much more could have been achieved in less time if their resources had been as bountiful as those of other lobbying groups in Washington, D.C. Their struggle was a deeply personal, transformative experience. Some were young students; others were nurturing new families. They took on the challenge of joining the resistance, not fully realizing that their commitment would eventually hold them back in their careers and affect their family life. In some cases, bitter intramural disputes shattered friendships. The exiled leaders of the MFP had to cope with economic survival. Some who joined the movement, including this author, had no idea that it would last for years and that it could plunge them into doubt and desperation. If only the immigrant Filipino community had responded to their agenda in large numbers. But apathy and fear were too embedded for the majority. Long-distance nationalism, it seems, was not a rallying call for all.

The exiles drew comfort from the knowledge that their allies in the homeland appreciated their contribution. They demonstrated the need for an offshore ally to support their home-based resistance. The Movement for a Free Philippines was not a household name among the Manila-based opposition groups. More well known were the leftist-oriented student groups Kabataang Makabayan (Nationalist Youth) and the Communist Party's NPA (New People's Army) guerrillas. But thanks to the constant references to Manglapus in the Philippine newspapers, "people knew him, not MFP," and that he was leading the anti-Marcos resistance in the United States, said Charles Avila.[11]

Perhaps one of their most enduring legacies is the lesson they taught U.S. foreign policy makers—that a small number of dedicated exile oppositionists can wield influence far beyond their tiny ranks. The United States lost its Philippine bases, and a generation of Filipinos who lived through the agony of the martial law regime are deeply aware that the U.S. government sided with a dictator. Never again would they allow foreign interests to trample their sovereignty. In the context of the Cold War, of competing ideologies, the U.S. government put its national interests—its bases and its business—first. But there were those in Congress who argued that the government was overzealous and underestimated the long-term consequences. Today, with the collapse of the Soviet Union, American foreign policy makers may perhaps avoid the inflexibility of Cold War imperatives. Marcos, as the saying goes, was an S.O.B., but he was "our S.O.B."—the United States would stand by him, no matter what.

Twenty-five years ago, *Time* magazine featured Corazon Aquino as its Person of the Year. By vanquishing a dictator, this widow who led the first People Power revolution introduced the model that would inspire the waves of people who tore down the Berlin Wall in 1989 and who massed at Tahrir Square in Cairo in 2011. The same magazine selected as its 2011 Person of the Year "The Protester—From the Arab Spring to Athens, from Occupy Wall Street to Moscow." By way of introduction, *Time* wrote: "history often emerges only in retrospect. Events become significant only when looking back."[12] Filipinos quickly took note of the historical antecedents of their own revolution and of these current upheavals. When the protesters in Egypt toppled a dictator, they started a global wave of dissent that engulfed other countries in the region and beyond. The protesters were encouraged in part by compatriots and like-minded sympathizers around the world. In this context, the exile Filipino oppositionists can truly say that they have been there and done that.

Notes

Preface

1. Heindl, "Transnational Political Activism," article abstract.
2. Sharp, *From Dictatorship to Democracy*, 44.

Chapter 1. The First Exiles

1. Karnow, *In Our Image*, 439.
2. The CSM was organized as a political party in 1968 by Manglapus and a number of associates. It advocated for social and economic reform based on Christian ethics. There were two major Philippine political parties at that time.
3. Manglapus, *Pen for Democracy*, xvii–xxiii.

Chapter 2. Rough Landings

1. Pacita and Raulito Manglapus interviews.
2. Fortich, *Escape!*, 152–56.
3. Maramba, *Six Modern Filipino Heroes*, 158.
4. Letter from Raoul Beloso to Manglapus, August 11, 1974. Copy in author's possession.
5. Letter to the Editor, *Filipino Reporter*, April 23, 1975, n.d. Copy in author's possession.
6. Copy of letter in author's possession.
7. Letter from Charles Maynes to Ambassador to the Philippines William Sullivan, April 21, 1975. Copy in author's possession.
8. Letter from Benjamin A. Fleck, Director of the Office of Philippine Affairs,

Department of State, to Steve Psinakis, June 30, 1976. Reproduced as appendix G in Manglapus, *Pen for Democracy*.

9. Maynes to Sullivan, April 21, 1975.

10. Charles Bartlett, "Diffidence Found in Policy on Philippines Reassuring," *Chicago Sun-Times*, May 10, 1975, 28.

11. Manglapus, *Pen for Democracy*, xvii.

12. Victor Lasky, *Never Complain, Never Explain: The Story of Henry Ford II* (New York: R. Marek, 1981), 208.

13. Manglapus, *Pen for Democracy*, xxiii; Lasky, *Never Complain*, 208.

14. Manglapus, *Pen for Democracy*, xxiv.

Chapter 3. Into the Land of the Fearful

1. "150 Names in Blacklist," *Philippine News*, May 24–30, 1973, 1.

2. Ibid.

3. Ibid.

4. "Baliao Defection Reactions Favorable," *Philippine News*, May 24–30, 1973, 1.

5. Ibid.

6. "Manglapus Exhorts Filipinos in US to Ignore FM Threats," *Philippine News*, May 14–30, 1973, 1.

7. Bonifacio Gillego, "The Spy Network of the Marcos Dictatorship in the USA," internal memorandum, Movement for a Free Philippines, 1982.

8. Fox Butterfield, "Former Aide Says Manila Plotted to Kill Him," *New York Times*, August 31, 1983, 6. When Ronald Reagan was elected president in 1981, he made good on his promise to Marcos that his administration would start cracking down on U.S.-based opposition groups. In preparation for the first grand jury proceedings, several agencies of the U.S. government had begun an "extremely sensitive investigation of the Movement for a Free Philippines. The documents comprise more than 1 ½ file drawers in Customs San Francisco . . . There are also files in Tucson and Phoenix, Arizona; Los Angeles, California; Washington, DC; New York; Boston; Hong Kong. The records consist of Reports of Investigations, Memorandum of Information Received, notes of surveillance, Grand Jury subpoenas, Grand Jury depositions, cables and classified reports regarding individuals and groups involved in the 'Movement for a Free Philippines' activities." Affidavit of John P. Simpson, Director of U.S. Customs Service, *John F. Leach v. U.S. Customs Service, U.S. Treasury Department*, Civil Action no. 85-1195, U.S. District Court for the District of Columbia. A reporter for the *Arizona Republic*, Leach requested the release of the documents through the Freedom of Information Act. His request was denied.

9. As quoted in Poole and Vanzi, *Revolution*, 269.

10. McCoy, *Anarchy of Families*, 429–30.

11. "For Filipino in Exile, the Long Wait Is Over," *New York Times*, March 5, 1986, A12.

12. "Marcos Is Said to Admit to Spy Activity in U.S.," *Washington Post*, July 16, 1986, A19.

13. In its special Fiftieth Anniversary Edition, the *Columbia Journalism Review*, a U.S. publication, chided *Fortune* for publishing a ten-page advertising supplement ("The Philippines: A New Role for Southeast Asia") in 1976 "without disclosing that the Marcos government had paid the magazine $183,000 to print the article, unlabeled as an advertisement." Brent Cunningham, "An Exercise in Humility: Fifty Years of Journalism's Lesser Angels," *Columbia Journalism Review*, November–December 2011, 30, available online at http://www.cjr.org/darts_and_laurels/darts_and_laurels_novdec2011.php (accessed Sept. 5, 2012).

14. Espiritu, *Five Faces*, 40.

15. In this same speech, Romulo expanded on "lawlessness" as one of the five reasons for imposing martial law: "The problem of lawlessness, anarchy and rampant criminality was a fourth. These conditions were aggravated by the existence of open as well as covert rebellions. As you recall conditions prior to martial law had deteriorated to a point that reminds one of certain portions of the United States where even walking on the street in broad daylight is fraught with physical danger. What was worse, the flouting of authority had developed in people a disdain for duty and order, so that even the matter of paying one's taxes or the proper customs duties became a game of circumventing of the law, with the willing connivance of the agents of the law." The other four reasons he cited were land reform, government corruption, government inefficiency, and the failure of institutions such as education, business, and "even the Church that were at loggerheads with the state, and with one another." The full speech is included in an MFP booklet, *NO: The New Society; A Prelude to Dictatorship by Raul S. Manglapus. YES: Our Democratic Revolution by Carlos P. Romulo* (New York: Movement for a Free Philippines, 1973).

16. Raul Manglapus interview.

17. Pacis, "Opposition in Absentia," 35.

18. Manglapus, *Pen for Democracy*, 16.

19. Espiritu, *Home Bound*, 80.

20. "Interview with an Exile," *America*, December 29, 1973, n.p.

Chapter 4. The Big Divide

1. See Quinsaat, *Letters in Exile*, pt. 2: "Exile and Exclusion," 35–96.

2. Yuchengco and Ciria-Cruz, "Filipino-American Community," 156.

3. "The Million Who Are There, but Have Not Quite Arrived," *The Economist*, January 25, 1986, 22. Apart from the "brain drain" caused by skilled Filipinos moving to the United States, the U.S. embassy in Manila collects about $26.9 million a year in visa fees, based on around eight hundred visa applications processed each day, according to U.S. Consul General Michael Schimmel at the opening of a new $50 million embassy annex on Roxas Boulevard. Rey O. Arcilla, "P1.183

Billion Just on Visa Fees," *Malaya*, May 3, 2011, A5. "That building is really a cash register," former Philippine senator Ralph Recto had remarked earlier. He suggested that the U.S. government should use part of the collected fees to fund social projects in the Philippines such as school buildings. "Philippines: A Cash Cow for the United States," *Filipino Reporter*, March 3, 2005, n.p.

4. See Allen, "Recent Immigration."

5. "The Million Who Are There," 22.

6. Ibid.

7. "The Asian American Vote in the 2008 Presidential Election: A Report of the Asian American Legal Defense and Education Fund," www.aaldef.org/docs/AALDEF2008ExitPollRpt.pdf (accessed Sept. 6, 2012).

8. McCallus, "Rhetoric of Ethnic Journalism," 18.

9. Allen, "Recent Immigration," 208.

Chapter 5. Martial Law and Beyond

1. "Inaugural Address of President Marcos, December 30, 1965," *Official Gazette*, available online at http://www.gov.ph/1965/12/30/inaugural-address-of-president-marcos-december-30-1965/ (accessed Sept. 6, 2012).

2. Bain, *Sitting in Darkness*, 4.

3. Karnow, *In Our Image*, 438. In addition, according to Raymond Bonner, $31 million was committed to settle Philippine veterans' claims, and $3.5 million for Imelda Marcos's Cultural Center; Bonner, *Waltzing*, 53.

4. In 1980, Reagan would order an FBI crackdown on anti-Marcos activists, mainly MFP leaders, as will be described in a later chapter.

5. Proclamation no. 1081, s. 1972, *Official Gazette*, available online at http://www.gov.ph/1972/09/21/proclamation-no-1081/ (accessed Sept. 16, 2012).

6. *New York Times*, March 2, 1978; *Washington Post*, April 11, 1978; as quoted in Psinakis, *Two Terrorists Meet*, 82, 80.

Chapter 6. Early Organizing

1. Schirmer, "Movement against U.S. Intervention," available online at http://groups.yahoo.com/group/anti_gma/message/1293 (accessed Sept. 6, 2012).

2. Ibid.

3. Gaerlan, "Boone Schirmer and the Early Days," available online at http://escholarship.org/uc/item/2mf4v5p5 (accessed Sept. 2, 2012).

4. Ibid.

5. Rene Cruz, "The KDP Story: The First Ten Years," *Ang Katipunan* 9, no. 8, Special Supplement (September 1983): 3, available online at http://pcdecal.wikispaces.com/file/view/ak-kdp-history.pdf (accessed Sept. 6, 2012).

6. Schirmer, "Movement against U.S. Intervention."

7. Letter from Daniel Boone Schirmer to the author, January 24, 1996.

8. Schirmer, "Movement against U.S. Intervention."

9. Rodriguez interview.

10. David interview.

11. Rodriguez interview.

12. Helen C. Toribio, "Dare to Struggle: The KDP and Filipino American Politics," in Ho, *Legacy to Liberation,* 34.

13. For a more extensive discussion of this subject, see Augusto Espiritu, "Journeys of Discovery and Difference: Transnational Politics and the Union of Democratic Filipinos," in Collet and Lien, *Transnational Politics,* 38–55.

14. Toribio, "Dare to Struggle," 38.

15. Letter from Manglapus to Bonifacio Gillego, April 30, 1985. Copy in author's possession.

16. Bonifacio Gillego, "Alliance with the Left," *Mr & Ms,* August 30–September 5, 1985, 13.

17. Bonifacio Gillego "Communists Are Neither Angels nor Devils Incarnate: A Rejoinder," *Mr & Ms,* November 22–28, 1985, n.p.

18. Clipping from *Washington Magazine,* n.d., n.p.

19. For a full list of MFP chapters, see appendix A.

20. Cipriano and Marina Espina interviews. Marina Espina is the author of *Filipinos in Louisiana* (New Orleans: Laborde, 1988).

21. Letter from Francisco Tatad to U.S. Representative Spark Matsunaga, March 21, 1975, as quoted in Psinakis, *Two Terrorists Meet,* 153.

22. Shain and Thompson, "Role of Political Exiles," 85.

23. Schirmer, "Movement against U.S. Intervention."

24. "In a Way NY Demos Projected the New Society," *Bulletin Today,* as quoted in Movement for a Free Philipines *News and Announcements,* February 1975, 10.

25. The ad, headlined "That the World May Know," appeared in the *New York Times* on September 27, 1973. It listed the first set of officers: Raul Manglapus, president; Dr. Renato Roxas, executive vice president; Jose Fuentecilla, secretary-general; Dr. Alfredo Arriola, treasurer; Antonio Valte, auditor; Regional Coordinators: East—Antonio Valte; Midwest—Dr. Norberto Portugal; West—Antonio Garcia; Regional Representatives to the Policy Board: East—Heherson Alvarez; Midwest—Marc Crudo; West—Ruperto Baliao; Committee Chairpersons: Sociopolitical action—Ruby von Oeyen; Finance—Dr. Edgardo Espiritu; Information—Antonio Garcia; Research & Development—Gerald Drummond; Education & Organization—Jun Atienza; Special Projects—Charlie Avila; Honorary Adviser—Salvador Araneta.

26. For statistics on Filipino physicians in the 1970s, see Mamot, *Foreign Medical Graduates,* 119; and Mejía, Pizurki, and Royston, *Physician and Nurse Migration,* 352–55.

27. Taca, "Steak Guerrillas," 62.

Chapter 7. Learning How to Lobby

1. "Senate, 44–41, Sends $2.3 Billion Aid Bill to the White House," *New York Times*, December 6, 1973, n.p.

2. U.S. Senate, Statement by Senator J. W. Fulbright on Introduction of a Bill to Revise the Foreign Military Aid and Sales Program, Senate Committee on Foreign Relations, *Foreign Military Sales and Assistance Act*, 93rd Cong., 1st sess., May 2, 1973, 2–3.

3. "For U.S., Still a 'Wide Reservoir of Good Will': President of Philippines Speaks His Mind," *U.S. News & World Report*, September 20, 1976, 65.

4. Bonner, *Waltzing*, 273.

5. Francis X. Clines, "Manila Says $1.1 Million Is Missing; Calls It U.S. Aid Fund Used by Marcos," *New York Times*, March 21, 1986, A6.

6. "U.S. Charges Marcoses Diverted AID Funds; $15 Million Allegedly Sent to Swiss Bank," *Washington Post*, November 30, 1989, A11.

7. U.S. House of Representatives, *Foreign Assistance Legislation for Fiscal Year 1985: Hearings before the Committee on Foreign Affairs*, 98th Cong., 2nd sess., vol. 5, 195.

8. U.S. House of Representatives, *Foreign Assistance and Related Programs Appropriations for 1985: Hearings before a Subcommittee of the Committee on Appropriations*, 98th Cong., 2nd sess., vol. 5, 162.

9. Hutchcroft, *Booty Capitalism*, 234, quoting Max Weber.

10. "Conclusion: Development Debacle," in *Development Debacle: The World Bank in the Philippines*, by Walden Bello, David Kinley, and Elaine Elinson (San Francisco: Institute for Food and Development Policy, 1982), 199.

11. "Pacific Panopticon," *New Left Review*, no. 16 (July–August 2002), 77, available online at http://www.focusweb.org/node/101 (accessed Sept. 16, 2012).

12. Walden Bello, "Challenges and Dilemmas of the Public Intellectual," acceptance speech at the Outstanding Public Scholar Award Panel, International Studies Association, 49th Annual Convention, San Francisco, California, March 27, 2008, available online at http://burawoy.berkeley.edu/Public%20Sociology,%20 Live/Bello/Challenges%20and%20Dilemmas%20of%20the%20Public%20Intellectual.pdf (accessed Sept. 7, 2012).

13. U.S. House of Representatives, *Human Rights in South Korea and the Philippines: Implications for U.S. Policy*, Hearings before the Subcommittee on International Organizations of the Committee on International Relations, 94th Cong., 1st sess., 312.

14. Raul Manglapus interview.

15. Robert Pear, "Foes of Marcos Gaining Listeners," *New York Times*, November 29, 1985, B14.

16. On September 20, 1974, Marcos was interviewed from Manila via satellite by several news organizations, including NBC in New York.

17. "Philippines Orders Inquiry on Soldiers Accused of Torture," *New York Times*, February 5, 1975, n.p.

18. Jack Anderson and Les Whitten, "Marcos Bribe Offer Cited by Witness," *Washington Post*, July 2, 1975, C7, reprinted in *Human Rights in South Korea and the Philippines*, 482.

19. For an extensive account of the Mijares case, see Psinakis, *Two Terrorists Meet*, 186–205.

Chapter 8. Down with Rhetoric!

1. Maramba, *Six Modern Filipino Heroes*, 154.

2. Thompson, *Anti-Marcos Struggle*, 85.

3. Jack Cheevers and Spencer A. Sherman, "The Palace Plot," *Mother Jones*, June 1983, 33.

4. Manglapus, *Pen for Democracy*, 175.

5. Gillego interview.

6. Raul Manglapus interview.

7. Alvarez interview.

8. Psinakis interview.

9. "15 Suspects Arrested," *Philippine Sunday Express*, December 30, 1979, n.p.

10. Maramba, *Six Modern Filipino Heroes*, 145–48.

11. Ortigas and Mayuga, *Revolutionary Odyssey*, 117–18.

12. Ortigas interview.

13. Gillego interview.

14. Note from Serge Osmena III to Bonifacio Gillego, n.d.

15. Letter from Raul Manglapus to Ferdinand Marcos, November 8, 1979.

16. Raul Manglapus interview.

17. Gillego interview.

18. Ibid.

19. Ibid.

20. Copy of dossier in author's possession.

21. U.S. House, *Foreign Assistance and Related Programs Appropriations for 1985*, 681.

22. Gillego interview.

23. Note from Bonifacio Gillego to Ralph Recto, January 12, 1978. Copy in author's possession.

24. Gillego interview.

25. John Sharkey, "The Marcos Mystery: Did the Philippine Leader Really Win U.S. Medals for Valor?" *Washington Post*, December 18, 1983, C1.

26. "Ferdinand Marcos: Hero or Fraud?," *Congressional Record* 129, no. 30 (March 11, 1983): 5070.

27. Sharkey, "Marcos Mystery."

28. Jeff Gerth, "Marcos's Wartime Role Discredited in U.S. Files," *New York Times*, January 23, 1986, 1.

29. Ibid.

30. Ibid.

31. Horacio Paredes, "Raul Manglapus Is Alive and Well and Doing Battle with the Enemy," *Mr & Ms*, December 23 and 30, 1983, n.p.

32. William Branigin, "Morale Low in Philippine Armed Forces," *Washington Post*, November 2, 1985, A19.

Chapter 9. The War of Words

1. "Tufts University Branch Cancels a Marcos Chair," *New York Times*, January 14, 1981, A17.

2. Shalom, "Promoting Ferdinand Marcos," 24.

3. Telegram from Michael Armacost to Assistant Secretary of State John Holdridge, Washington, D.C., July 22, 1982, marked "Confidential," obtained through the Freedom of Information Act.

4. McCallus, "Rhetoric of Ethnic Journalism," 140.

5. Ibid., 141.

6. Doroy Valencia, newspaper clipping from the *Times Journal*, n.d., n.p.

7. U.S.-based publicists representing foreign governments are required to register their activities with the Department of Justice in Washington, D.C. Their filings are open to the public. International Counselors Ltd. of Washington, D.C., was paid $205,666 for the twelve-month period ending August 3, 1980, for "communications and media relations . . . in connection with President Marcos' visit to Honolulu to address the American Newspaper Publishers Association." Doremus & Co. of New York was paid $368,400 for the nine-month period ending February 18, 1979, "to counsel visiting [Philippine] foreign dignitaries with a communications program . . . Registrant disseminated press releases, newsletters, and other printed matter to newspapers, press services, public officials and others covering a wide range of topics such as the convening of the legislative assembly and the end of martial law, a visit to the U.S. by the Philippine Foreign Minister, a defense against charges of human rights violations, and other news in the areas of politics, economics and culture."

8. Lynn Rosellini, "Marcos Defends His Rights and Spending Records," *New York Times*, September 18, 1982, 3.

9. Here is a sampling of the headlines about the welcoming ceremonies at the White House on September 16, 1982: "Reagan Praises Marcos as a Voice for Moderation," *New York Times*; "Marcos Welcomed with Warm Praise," *Washington Post*; "Marcos: U.S. Trustee against Second Dark Age," *Washington Times*; "Marcos Arrives; Scolds U.S.," *San Francisco Chronicle*; "Reagan Welcomes Marcos to U.S.," *Los Angeles Times*.

10. "U.S. Media Give Extensive Treatment to Visit," *Filipino Chronicle*, September 30, 1982, 6.

11. McCallus, "Rhetoric of Ethnic Journalism," 165.

12. Newspaper clipping from the *Filipino Chronicle*, n.d., n.p.

13. During the martial law years, protest groups that formed across the country issued their own publications, among them *Silayan* and *Makibaka* (from the National Committee for the Restoration of Civil Liberties in the Philippines, San Francisco, Calif.), *Bangon* (Ann Arbor, Mich.), *Pahayag* (Honolulu), the *Philippines Information Bulletin* (Cambridge, Mass.), and *Tambuli* (Chicago, Ill.). In most cases, these were more like newsletters, with much lower circulations than tabloid or broadsheet newspapers, and just as limited in life span.

14. "Are We Prepared to Meet History's Judgement?" *Philippine News*, April 10–16, 1975, 4, as quoted in Vergara, *Pinoy Capital*, 120.

15. See also Pat Ferguson, "Marcos Foe Files Bankruptcy," *San Francisco Examiner*, March 20, 1985, A1.

16. U.S. State Department telegram from Richard Murphy to Richard Holbrook, head of the Bureau of East Asian and Pacific Affairs, August 16, 1979, marked "Secret," obtained through the Freedom of Information Act.

17. Vergara, *Pinoy Capital*, 117. Cruz, "KDP Story," details the group's community activities in support of Filipino doctors, nurses, elderly tenants, and agricultural trainees.

18. Its editor, Libertito Pelayo, had earlier worked as a journalist in Manila.

19. "Opposition Undercut by Warm RP-US Ties," *Filipino Reporter*, December 18–24, 1982, n.p.

20. Bonner, *Waltzing*, 317.

21. Quoted ibid.

22. "An Amnesty International USA Statement on Human Rights Violations in the Philippines—Torture, Extra-Judicial Executions and Political Imprisonment," *New York Times*, September 17, 1982, n.p.

Chapter 10. Reviving the Opposition

1. Ortiz and Alvarez interviews.

2. Quoted in Thompson, *Anti-Marcos Struggle*, 90.

3. Quoted in Psinakis, *Two Terrorists Meet*, 19.

4. Typewritten manifesto. Copy in author's possession.

5. "Marcos Speech before ASTA," *Bulletin Today*, October 20, 1980, 16.

6. For the full list, see "Salonga, 3 Other Ex-Senators in U.S. Held; FM Links Them to ASTA Blast," *Bulletin Today*, October 21, 1980, n.p.

7. "Marcos Aide Fearful of New Group of Foes," *Washington Post*, October 25, 1980, A20.

8. Thompson, *Anti-Marcos Struggle*, 89.

9. Letter from Raul Manglapus to Steve Psinakis, January 27, 1981. Copy in author's possession.

10. Letter from Steve Psinakis to Raul Manglapus, January 30, 1981. Copy in author's possession.

11. Quoted in Maramba, *Six Modern Filipino Heroes*, 46–47. Jose Rizal, the country's foremost national hero, led a movement of Filipino students in Spain that advocated reforms for the Philippines. This angered the Spanish colonial rulers, who executed him on December 30, 1896, in Manila.

12. Ibid.

13. Shain and Thompson, "Role of Political Exiles," 81.

14. Thompson, *Anti-Marcos Struggle*, 110.

15. Letter from Raul Manglapus to Mrs. Aurora Aquino, mother of Benigno Aquino, September 7, 1983. Copy in author's possession.

16. Apiado interview.

17. Note from Jose Calderon to Bonifacio Gillego, December 27, 1983. Copy in author's possession.

18. "Marcos Losing Credibility of Filipinos, Yet Everything Hangs on His Decisions," *Wall Street Journal*, October 18, 1983, n.p. The story also reported that since the murder of Aquino, "Filipinos have taken hundreds of millions of dollars out of the country. Skittish foreign companies won't invest. And foreign bankers, who will have to lend more to keep the Philippines solvent, say they won't ante up until the political turmoil subsides."

19. Abraham Sarmiento, who represented the former president, Diosdado Macapagal, was a former delegate to and vice president of the Constitutional Convention in 1971–72 and currently secretary-general of the Liberal Party. The four former senators—Jose Diokno, Lorenzo Tanada, Manglapus, and Salonga—were singled out in a study of Philippine politics as outstanding examples of men who did not fit the usual pattern of "conniving, self-serving politicians." In their long careers, "they were also animated by human rights, public policy issues, significant legal questions, and philosophical dilemmas. They were not bought or manipulated men; nor were they apparently forever scheming how to buy and manipulate others . . . All have been described as nationalists." Benedict J. Tria Kerkvliet, "Toward a More Comprehensive Analysis of Philippine Politics: Beyond the Patron-Client, Factional Framework," *Journal of Southeast Asian Studies* 26, no. 2 (September 1995): 412.

20. John McLean, "Opposition Prepares for Marcos Downfall," *South China Morning Post* (Hong Kong), April 6, 1984, 20.

21. Unidentified article from *Panorama*, April 1984, as quoted in "What to Expect from the 1984 Elections," *MFP Newsletter*, May 1984, 12.

22. Notes from the meeting written by Bonifacio Gillego. The others present at the meeting from March 12 to 18, 1983, were Eugenio Lopez Jr.; Luis Jose, the secretary-general of the CSM; and Emmanuel Cruz of the CSM. Handwritten notes in author's possession.

23. Excerpt from a five-page letter from Raul Manglapus to Ferdinand Marcos, November 8, 1979 . Copies were sent to opposition groups in Manila, where it was reproduced and distributed.

24. Paredes, "Raul Manglapus Is Alive and Well."

Chapter 11. Reviewing the Decade

1. Raul Manglapus, speech before the delegates, May 14, 1983. Typewritten copy in author's possession.

2. "Movement in US Ousts Manglapus," *Manila Bulletin*, May 17, 1983, n.p.

3. Tom Achacoso, "A Time for Reassessment" (1983), 15 pages. Achacoso served as labor attaché at the Philippine embassy in Saudi Arabia in 1980–81, where Imelda Marcos's brother Benjamin Romualdez was ambassador. He defected to the MFP in June 1981.

4. Gregor, "Key Role of the U.S. Bases," 10.

5. Jane Mayer, "Right-Wing Thinkers Push Ideas," *Wall Street Journal*, December 7, 1984, n.p.

6. Gregor, *U.S. and the Philippines*, 78.

7. Marjorie Niehaus, "Philippine Internal Conditions: Issues for U.S. Policy," Congressional Research Service, Issue Brief no. IB82102, update of May 26, 1983.

8. "Visit of President Marcos," section on "Current Political & Economic Situation," Department of State background paper, April 19–26, 1980, marked "Secret," obtained through the Freedom of Information Act.

Chapter 12. "It's Not All Greek to Me"

1. Leslie Guevara and L. A. Chung, "S.F. Arrest of Marcos Foe Stuns Filipino Community," *San Francisco Chronicle*, July 7, 1987, n.p.

2. Phil Bronstein, "Philippine Anti-Marcos 'Hero' Faces Prosecution in the U.S.," *San Francisco Examiner*, February 4, 1988, n.p.; reproduced as appendix 14 in Psinakis, *A Country Not Even His Own*, 286.

3. United States District Court for the Northern District of California, search warrant, *United States of America v. The Premises Known as 545 Darien Way*, San Francisco, California, Docket No. 3-81-2080MW.

4. Lloyd Shearer, "Extortion in High Places," *Parade*, March 2, 1975, n.p. In his press statement, Eugenio estimated his companies' worth at $400 million. The full statement appears as appendix 7 in Psinakis, *A Country Not Even His Own*, 260.

5. Psinakis, *A Country Not Even His Own*, 261.

6. Psinakis, *Two Terrorists Meet*, 157.

7. Ibid.

8. The drama of this event is described in detail by Stu Cohen, "The Great Escape," *Boston Phoenix*, November 8, 1977, n.p., as published in Psinakis, *Two Terrorists Meet*, 158–67.

9. Cheevers and Sherman, "Palace Plot," 34.

10. Ibid., 35; Psinakis, *Two Terrorists Meet*, 29.

11. Taca, "Steak Guerrillas," 63.

12. Ibid., 66. "Bayan Ko" (My Country) was the anthem of choice for opposition groups in Manila during mass rallies. The Detroit group had MFP members attending the event.

13. As quoted in "Terrorist or Hero," *Philippine News*, May 17–23, 1989, n.p.

14. Email from Coco Taca to author, April 16, 2011.

15. Poole and Vanzi, *Revolution*, 298.

16. *United States of America v. Steven Elias Psinakis and Charles Avila*, Case no. CR 86-1064 RHS, U.S. District Court, Northern California, Affidavit of Victor Burns Lovely, Jr., May 13, 1988. The *Arizona Republic*, a newspaper based in Phoenix, published details of the training that Lovely said he and others underwent at three sites in the Arizona desert. Based on records, "including an FBI report classified 'secret' and other investigative reports," the newspaper wrote that four groups of Filipinos trained between November 1979 and 1980. The chief trainer was a retired U.S. Special Forces sergeant from Tucson named Gregory Kandziora. See "Philippine Bombers Were Trained in State," *Arizona Republic*, February 19, 1984, n.p.

17. *U.S. v. Psinakis and Avila*, Affidavit of Victor Burns Lovely, Jr.

18. Katherine Bishop, "Court Case Links Aquino Allies to Bomb-Making," *New York Times*, December 15, 1988, 4.

19. *U.S. v. Psinakis and Avila*, Memorandum of Points and Authorities in Support of Defendant's Motion No. 1: To Dismiss the Indictment for Discriminatory Prosecution, May 13, 1988, 28.

20. Richard Martin, "Reviving Scenes from a Revolution," *Insight*, February 20, 1989, 34.

21. Alvarez was elected senator after being named Aquino's minister of agrarian affairs in her first cabinet.

22. Martin, "Reviving Scenes," 35.

23. *U.S. v. Psinakis and Avila*, Memorandum of Points and Authorities.

Chapter 13. A Man for Many Seasons

1. James B. Reuter, "At 3:00 A.M.," *Philippine Star*, August 7, 1999, n.p., as quoted in Bonner, *Waltzing*, 143.

2. Raul Manglapus, "Fort Santiago—Plus Somewhat More: One Man's Little War Story" (unpublished ms., 9 pages, n.d.).

3. Ibid.; Reuter, "At 3:00 A.M."

4. Pacis, "Opposition in Absentia," 98.

5. Letter from Manglapus to David Martinez, Chairman, Los Angeles MFP Chapter, August 10, 1979. Copy in author's possession.

6. Hilarion Henares Jr., "Make My Day: Thank God, Manglapus Was in USA during Martial Law," *Philippine Daily Inquirer*, April 6, 1987, n.p.

7. Jose Rizal Memorial Lecture, delivered at the 1987 National Conference of the Philippine Center of International PEN, reprinted in *Mr & Ms*, June 5–11, 1987, 12.

8. Tom Buckley, "Footnotes before the Footlights: Premiere in Hawaii," *New York Times*, July 7, 1974, 36.

9. Letter from Arthur Zich to Jack Kroll, June 1, 1974. Copy in author's possession.

10. Hilarion Henares Jr., "Make My Day: Raul's 'Yanky Panky,'" *Philippine Post*, August 10, 1999, n.p., available online at http://benmaynigo.blogspot.com/2010/07/rauls-yanky-panky.html (accessed Sept. 13, 2012).

11. Buckley, "Footnotes before the Footlights."

12. Letter from Raul Manglapus to Ferdinand Marcos, September 28, 1979. Copy in author's possession.

13. Bonner, *Waltzing*, 208.

14. U.S. House of Representatives, *Hearings before the Subcommittee on Future Foreign Policy Research and Development of the Committee on International Relations*, 94th Cong., 1st sess., November 18 and December 10, 1975; January 28, March 8, April 7, and May 18, 1970, 181.

15. Karnow, *In Our Image*, 332.

16. Seth Mydans, "U.S. 'Father Image' Is Blamed for Low Filipino Self-Esteem," *New York Times*, December 28, 1987, A6.

17. Seth Mydans, "Raul Manglapus, 80, Dies; Power in Post-Marcos Era," *New York Times*, July 27, 1999, n.p.

18. It was from Clark Air Base that Reagan had dispatched a helicopter on February 26, 1986, to fly Marcos, his wife, and General Ver out of the Presidential Palace, rescuing them from the angry throngs of the People Power uprising.

19. Clyde Haberman, "The Return of an Exile: 'It's the Greatest Story,'" *New York Times*, March 1, 1986, 7.

20. Mydans, "Raul Mangalpus, 80, Dies."

21. Martin Weil, "Raul S. Manglapus, Former Foreign Secretary of Philippines, Dies at 80," *Washington Post*, July 26, 1999, B6.

Epilogue

1. As quoted in Manglapus, "Christian Force," 4 n. 13.

2. Benigno S. Aquino Jr., "What's Wrong with the Philippines?," *Foreign Affairs* 46, no. 4 (July 1968): 770.

3. As quoted in Bonner, *Waltzing*, 271, citing statistics from the 1978 *Far Eastern Economic Review Yearbook*, 53, and *The World Bank Philippine Poverty Report: The Confidential First-Draft Version Obtained by the Congress Task Force and Counterspy Magazine*, 25.

4. James Fallows, "A Damaged Culture: A New Philippines?," *Atlantic Monthly*, November 1, 1987, 56, available online at http://www.theatlantic.com/technology/archive/1987/11/a-damaged-culture-a-new-philippines/7414/ (accessed Sept. 13, 2012). This feature caused a furor—for and against its thesis—among scholars of Philippine history. A sample of their opinions can be seen in the "Letters to the Editor" column of the magazine in the March 1988 issue. The reference to Fallows's piece is included here because the magazine has an influential readership among American policy makers.

5. McCoy, *Policing America's Empire*, 403. See also Raissa Robles, "Aquino Leads Push for Truth Body," *South China Morning Post*, September 28, 1999, n.p. On September 25, 1992, a U.S. federal court in Honolulu, ruling in a class action suit, ordered the Marcos estate to compensate 9,539 victims of human rights violations under martial law. In July 2004, however, the Philippine government said that the court ruling to transfer $40 million in compensation payments from $684 million in Marcos assets found in Swiss banks could not be enforced against the Philippines because it was "a sovereign state outside the jurisdiction of the U.S. court." As of the first week of March 2011, the plaintiffs in the class action suit were scheduled to begin receiving $1,000 per person from another settlement of the case separate from the Honolulu ruling, which is being resolved. The funds were to come from a $10 million estate in Texas and Colorado found to have been bought with Marcos money. There are 7,526 plaintiffs eligible for this lawsuit. Two other cases in Singapore and New York involving a total of $68 million are also being concluded. Seth Mydans, "First Payments Are Made to Victims of Marcos Rule," *New York Times*, March 1, 2011, n.p.

6. In the elections for a new Congress, Manglapus was elected senator, but he vacated his seat when President Aquino named him foreign secretary; she named Alvarez secretary of agrarian reform in her first cabinet, after which he was elected senator; Osmena III was also elected to the Senate; Gillego and Daza were both elected to the House; Avila was elected mayor of his hometown of Tanauan in the province of Leyte.

7. Viernes and Domingo, both born in the United States (Viernes was the son of a Filipino father and an American mother), are examples of second-generation Filipinos who became anti-Marcos activists. As officers of the Seattle-based Alaska Cannery Workers Association–International Longshore and Warehouse Union, they led the passage of a resolution at the union's international 1981 convention in Hawaii condemning the anti-labor practices of Marcos's martial law regime. That led to a high-level union delegation (which included Viernes) to look into the plight of workers in the Philippines. In 1982, both were shot at their Local 37 union office in Seattle. Three gang members and a union boss were sentenced to life for the murders. In 1989 a U.S. federal jury "found not only that the Marcoses had been negligent in failing to control agents of their [American-based] intelligence network . . . but also that the Marcoses had actually been part of a conspiracy

that resulted in the slayings" ("Marcos's Estate and His Widow Are Held Liable in 2 U.S. Killings," *New York Times*, December 17, 1989, A36). See also Thomas Churchill, *Triumph over Marcos: A Story Based on the Lives of Gene Viernes and Silme Domingo, Filipino American Cannery Union Organizers, Their Assassin, and the Trial That Followed* (Greensboro, N.C.: Open Hand Publications, 1994).

8. Manglapus, *Pen for Democracy*, 176.

9. David Camroux, handout provided to the participants in a session at the Association of Asian Studies Annual Conference, Honolulu, March 31–April 4, 2011, summarizing his article "Nationalizing Transnationalism? The Philippine State and the Filipino Diaspora," *Les Études du CERI*, no. 152 (December 2008), n.p.

10. Malcolm Gladwell, "Small Change: Why the Revolution Will Not Be Tweeted," *New Yorker*, October 4, 2010, available online at http://www.newyorker.com/reporting/2010/10/04/101004fa_fact_gladwell (accessed Sept. 13, 2012).

11. Avila interview.

12. Rick Stengel, "Person of the Year Introduction," *Time*, Wednesday, December 14, 2011, available online at http://www.time.com/time/specials/packages/article/0,28804,2101745_2102139,00.html (accessed Sept. 13, 2012).

Bibliography

Allen, James P. "Recent Immigration from the Philippines and Filipino Communities in the United States." *Geographical Review* 67, no. 2 (April 1977): 195–208.

Asian American Federation of New York. "Census Profile: New York City's Filipino American Population." New York: Asian American Federation of New York Census Information Center, 2004.

Bain, David Haward. *Sitting in Darkness: Americans in the Philippines.* New York: Penguin Books, 1984.

Bello, Madge, and Vincent Reyes. "Filipino Americans and the Marcos Overthrow: The Transformation of Political Consciousness." *Amerasia Journal* 13, no. 1 (1986–87): 73–83.

Bonner, Raymond. *Waltzing with a Dictator: The Marcoses and the Making of American Policy.* New York: Times Books, 1987.

Bonus, Rick. *Locating Filipino Americans: Ethnicity and the Cultural Politics of Space.* Philadelphia: Temple University Press, 2000.

Collet, Christian, and Pei-te Lien, eds. *The Transnational Politics of Asian Americans.* Philadelphia: Temple University Press, 2009.

Cuevas-Hewitt, Marco. "The Figure of the 'Fil-Whatever': Trans-Pacific Social Movements and the Rise of Radical Cosmopolitanism." *World Anthropologies Network E-Journal* 5/6 (2010): 97–127. http://www.ram-wan.net/documents/05_e_Journal/journal-5/6-cuevas.pdf (accessed Sept. 2, 2012).

Espiritu, Augusto Fauni. *Five Faces of Exile: The Nation and Filipino American Intellectuals.* Stanford, Calif.: Stanford University Press, 2003.

Espiritu, Yen Le. *Home Bound: Filipino American Lives across Cultures, Communities, and Countries.* Berkeley: University of California Press, 2003.

Fortich, Chic. *Escape! Charito Planas: Her Story.* Quezon City: New Day Publishers, 1991.

Gaerlan, Barbara S. "Boone Schirmer and the Early Days of the *Philippines Information Bulletin,* Friends of the Filipino People, and the Philippines Program at Goddard-Cambridge." Philippines/Schirmer Series, UCLA Center for Southeast Asian Studies, UCLA International Institute, University of California, Los Angeles, 2006.

Gregor, A. James. "The Key Role of the U.S. Bases in the Philippines." Asian Studies Center Backgrounder, no. 7. Washington, D.C.: The Heritage Foundation, January 10, 1984.

———. *The U.S. and the Philippines: A Challenge to a Special Relationship.* Washington, D.C.: Heritage Foundation, 1983.

Heindl, Brett Sheridan. "Transnational Political Activism in American Cuban, Jewish, and Irish Communities." Ph.D. diss., Syracuse University, 2007. Pro-Quest (AAT 3281721).

Ho, Fred, ed. *Legacy to Liberation: Politics and Culture of Revolutionary Asian Pacific America.* San Francisco: Big Red Media, 2000.

Hutchcroft, Paul D. *Booty Capitalism: The Politics of Banking in the Philippines.* Ithaca, N.Y.: Cornell University Press, 1998.

Ignacio, Emily Noelle. *Building Diaspora: Filipino Community Formation on the Internet.* New Brunswick, N.J.: Rutgers University Press, 2005.

Karnow, Stanley. *In Our Image: America's Empire in the Philippines.* New York: Random House, 1989.

Mamot, Patricio R. *Foreign Medical Graduates in America.* Springfield, Ill.: Charles C. Thomas, 1974.

Manglapus, Raul S. "The Christian Force: A Manifesto to the Filipino People." Washington, D.C.: Movement for a Free Philippines, 1979.

———. *A Pen for Democracy: A Decade of Articles, Speeches, Letters, Interviews, and Committee Testimony Published in the International Press and the U.S. Congressional Record in the Tradition of the Filipino Democrats a Century Ago.* Washington, D.C.: Movement for a Free Philippines, 1983.

Manglapus, Raul S., and Carlos P. Romulo. *NO: The New Society; A Prelude to Dictatorship. YES: Our Democratic Revolution.* New York: Movement for a Free Philippines, 1973.

Maramba, Asuncion David, ed. *Six Modern Filipino Heroes.* Manila: Anvil Publishing, 1993.

McCallus, Joseph P. "The Rhetoric of Ethnic Journalism: The Filipino American Press and Its Washington, D.C. Audience." Ph.D. diss., Catholic University of America, 1987.

McCoy, Alfred W. *An Anarchy of Families: State and Family in the Philippines.* Madison: University of Wisconsin Press, 2009.

———. *Policing America's Empire: The United States, the Philippines, and the Rise of the Surveillance State.* Madison: University of Wisconsin Press, 2009.

Mejía, Alfonso, Helena Pizurki, and Erica Royston. *Physician and Nurse Migra-*

tion: Analysis and Policy Implications; Report of a WHO Study. Geneva: World Health Organization, 1979.

Nadal, Kevin L. *Filipino American Psychology: A Collection of Personal Narratives*. Bloomington, Ind.: Author House, 2009.

Okamura, Jonathan Y. *Imagining the Filipino American Diaspora: Transnational Relations, Identities, and Communities*. New York: Garland Publishing, 1998.

Ortigas, Gaston Z., and Sylvia L. Mayuga. *A Revolutionary Odyssey: The Life and Times of Gaston Z. Ortigas*. Manila: Anvil Publishing, 1994.

Pacis, David Ramon Aguila. "The Opposition in Absentia: Philippine Political Exiles in the United States during the Marcos Regime, 1972–86." A.B. thesis, Harvard University, 1993.

The Philippines. Special Issue, *Bulletin of Concerned Asian Scholars* 22, no. 4 (1990).

Poole, Fred, and Max Vanzi. *Revolution in the Philippines: The United States in a Hall of Cracked Mirrors*. New York: McGraw-Hill, 1984.

Psinakis, Steve E. *A Country Not Even His Own*. Manila: Anvil, 2008.

———. *Two Terrorists Meet*. San Francisco: Alchemy Books, 1991.

Quinsaat, Jesse, ed. *Letters in Exile: An Introductory Reader on the History of Pilipinos in America*. Los Angeles: UCLA Asian American Studies Center, 1976.

Rafael, Vicente L. *White Love and Other Events in Filipino History*. Durham, N.C.: Duke University Press, 2000.

Schirmer, Daniel B. "The Movement against U.S. Intervention in the Philippines: A Sketch." Paper presented at a conference in New York City called by the Campaign to End U.S. Intervention in the Philippines, March 4, 1989.

Shain, Yossi. "Ethnic Diasporas and U.S. Foreign Policy." *Political Science Quarterly* 109, no. 5 (Winter 1994/95): 811–41.

Shain, Yossi, and Mark Thompson. "The Role of Political Exiles in Democratic Transitions: The Case of the Philippines." *Journal of Developing Societies* 6, no. 1 (1990): 71–86.

Shalom, Stephen R. "Promoting Ferdinand Marcos." *Bulletin of Concerned Asian Scholars* 22, no. 4 (1990): 20–26.

Sharp, Gene. *From Dictatorship to Democracy: A Conceptual Framework for Liberation*. Boston: Albert Einstein Institution, 2002.

Strobel, Leny Mendoza. *Coming Full Circle: The Process of Decolonization among Post-1965 Filipino-Americans*. Manila: Giraffe Books.

Taca, Arturo. "Steak Guerrillas." Unpublished memoir, 1997. 131 pages.

Thompson, Mark R. *The Anti-Marcos Struggle: Personalistic Rule and Democratic Transition in the Philippines*. Quezon City: New Day Publishers, 1996.

United States of America v. Steven Elias Psinakis and Charles Avila. U.S. District Court, Northern District of California, Case no. CR 86-1064 RHS.

U.S. House of Representatives. *Foreign Assistance Legislation for Fiscal Year 1985: Hearings before the Committee on Foreign Affairs*. Pt. 5: *Hearings and Markup before the Subcommittee on Asian and Pacific Affairs of the Committee on Foreign Affairs.* 98th Cong., 2nd sess., February 6, 7, 22, 23, and 28, 1984.

———. *Foreign Assistance Legislation for Fiscal Years 1986–87: Hearings before the Committee on Foreign Affairs. Pt. 5: Hearings and Markup before the Subcommittee on Asian and Pacific Affairs of the Committee on Foreign Affairs.* 99th Cong., 1st sess., February 20, 27, and 28; March 5, 6, 12, and 20, 1985.

———. *Reconciling Human Rights and U.S. Security Interests in Asia: Hearings before the Subcommittees on Asian and Pacific Affairs and on Human Rights and International Organizations of the Committee on Foreign Affairs.* 97th Cong., 2nd sess., August 10; September 21, 22, 28, and 29; December 3, 9, and 15, 1982.

———. *The Situation and Outlook in the Philippines: Hearings before the Subcommittee on Asian and Pacific Affairs of the Committee on Foreign Affairs.* 98th Cong., 2nd sess., September 20 and October 4, 1984.

———. *United States–Philippines Relations and the New Base and Aid Agreement: Hearings before the Subcommittee on Asian and Pacific Affairs of the Committee on Foreign Affairs.* 98th Cong., 1st sess., June 17, 23, and 28, 1983.

———. *U.S. Policy toward the Philippines: Hearing before the Subcommittees on Asian and Pacific Affairs and on Human Rights and International Organizations of the Committee on Foreign Affairs.* 97th Cong., 1st sess., November 18, 1981.

U.S. Senate. *Extradition Act of 1981: Hearing before the Committee on the Judiciary.* 97th Cong., 1st sess., on S. 1639, October 14, 1981.

———. *The Situation in the Philippines: A Staff Report, Prepared for the Committee on Foreign Relations.* 98th Cong., 2nd sess., October 1984.

Vergara, Benito M., Jr. *Pinoy Capital: The Filipino Nation in Daly City.* Philadelphia: Temple University Press, 2009.

Yuchengco, Mona Lisa, and Rene P. Ciria-Cruz. "The Filipino-American Community: New Roles and Challenges." In *The Philippines: New Directions in Domestic Policy and Foreign Relations,* edited by David G. Timberman, 155–73. New York: Asia Society, 1998.

Interviews

Alvarez, Heherson. November 17, 1995, Manila.

Apiado, Orlando. January 11, 1996, New York.

Avila, Charles. November 17, 1995, Manila.

Constantino, Alan. June 28, 1996, New York.

Crucillo, Wilfredo. November 9, 1995, Manila.

David, Amado. June 27, 1996, New York.

Espina, Cipriano. February 14, 1996, New Orleans.

Espina, Marina. February 14, 1996, New Orleans.

Gillego, Bonifacio. November 9, 1995, Manila.

Hewitt, Esther Soriano. June 27, 1996, New York.

Lachica, Eric. June 27, 1996, New York.
Manglapus, Pacita. November 14, 1995, Manila.
Manglapus, Raul. November 14, 1995, Manila.
Manglapus, Raulito. November 14, 1995, Manila.
Ortigas, Fluellen. November 11, 1995, Manila.
Ortiz, Jose. November 17, 1995, Manila.
Pena, Manuel. November 14 and 24, 1995.
Psinakis, Steve. December 2, 1999, Manila.
Rodriguez, Therese. June 28, 1996, New York.

Newspapers and Magazines Cited

U.S. newspapers: *Arizona Republic, Asian Wall St. Journal, New York Times, Wall Street Journal, Washington Post.* The *San Jose Mercury News* won the 1986 Pulitzer Prize in International Reporting for its series on "Hidden Billions" (June 23 to 25, 1985), an account of the Marcos holdings in the United States.

U.S. magazines: *Atlantic Monthly, Columbia Journalism Review, Fortune, Insight, Mother Jones, Newsweek, Time.*

U.S.-based Philippine newspapers: *Filipino Chronicle, Filipino Reporter, Philippine News.*

Manila-based newspapers and magazines: *Bulletin Today, Malaya, Mr & Ms, Philippine Star, Times Journal, We Forum.*

The *Economist* (London).

Far East Economic Review (Hong Kong).

South China Morning Post (Hong Kong).

Acknowledgments

This book has focused on the exploits of selected people who, by virtue of their leadership roles, embodied the struggle of leading an opposition movement. Behind them were many scores of followers, too numerous to name. But they were just as dedicated, driven by the same ideals as their leaders. They too shouldered burdens and carried on bravely.

Among the exceptional individuals who figured prominently in this account, two stand high above the others. They are Raul Manglapus and Bonifacio "Boni" Gillego. As the first secretary-general of the Movement for a Free Philippines, I witnessed at first hand the truly remarkable manner in which Raul, under personally trying circumstances, held together the often fractious, restless bands of his followers. While I was doing the research on this book, he made his most private papers available to me at his Ayala Alabang home in Manila. They covered the fourteen years of his exile in the United States.

Boni likewise kept a record of his exile years. And what a record—ten boxes of documents, from greeting cards to sales receipts, from secret memos to smuggled letters and meeting agendas, that in many ways traced the ebb and flow of that period. I had thought that my own collection of documents, which filled two four-drawer steel cabinets, contained enough primary documents to suit my needs. But Boni's trove was overwhelming and a most precious resource.

Beyond the physical objects that truly notable men leave for more historians to study, it is their legacy that endures. We owe them much.

Movement for a Free Philippines Chapters and Chairpersons (as of 1979)

International

Australia

    Canberra   Ian Swords

Canada

    Edmonton   Alex Juan

    Hamilton   John Glenn

    Montreal   Fred Magallanes

    Toronto   Efigenio S. Doroteo

France

    Paris   Sid Fabrico

Italy

    Rome   Tomas Concepcion

Japan

    Tokyo   Thelma Wakamiya

Saudi Arabia

    Riyadh   Maton Lucman Jr.

United States

Alaska

Anchorage	Millie James
Fairbanks	Dave Vaughn

Arizona

Phoenix	Sam Buot

California

Berkeley	Pete Fernandez
Brea	Gregorio Climaco
Carson City	Antonio Canon
Cerritos	Fr. Peter Ferrer
Culver City	Romy Anotes
Fresno	Jose Ayala
Gardena	Roy Gorre
Hayward	Jonathan de Guzman
Long Beach	Leony Gonzales
Los Angeles	Carlos Robes
Monterey	Vince Julio
Oxnard	Efren Gorre
San Fernando	Louie Eugenio
San Jose	John Gonzales
San Francisco	Presy Psinakis
Santa Clara	Guillermo Espinosa
South San Francisco Bay Area	Lou Clemente
West Covina	Eli Swing
West Los Angeles	Gamie Pilapil

Hawaii

Honolulu	Dr. Ruben Mallari

Illinois

Chicago

Abad Santos Chapter	Greg Manabat
Arayat Chapter	Meliton Tarus
Bataan Chapter	Lucia Afurung
Biak Na Bato Chapter	Benny San Juan
Corregidor Chapter	Cesar Arellano
Dapitan Chapter	Cris Abasolo
Freedom Chapter	Dale Pontius
Katipunan Chapter	Joe Trinidad

Mactan Chapter	Dr. Enrique Villalon
Malolos Chapter	Dr. Nestor Gatmaitan
Mecca Youth Chapter	Jocela Trinidad
Mecca I Chapter	Perla Rigor
Mecca II Chapter	Max Montayre
Mecca III Chapter	Diosdado Macapagal
Mecca IV Chapter	Andy Deconia
Mecca V Chapter	Al Williams
Tirad Pass Chapter	Roberto Roque
Downers Grove	Ener Sampang
Normal	Michael Matejka
Northbrook	Dr. Ronnie Paras
West Springs	Dr. Felicitas Tobias

Indiana

Gary	Ernie Hernandez

Kentucky

Hopkinsville	Bob Manlavi

Louisiana

New Orleans	Cipriano Espina Jr.

Massachusetts

Boston	Dr. Felipe Martin Suva

Michigan

Detroit	Zar Manzilla

Minnesota

St. Paul	Gary King

Missouri

St. Louis	Dr. Jose Vijungco

New Jersey

Jersey City	Winston Bontigao
Trenton	Felix Garcia

New York

New York	Manoling Maravilla
Rochester	Fernando Tinio

Ohio

    Bowling Green   R. A. Sanchez
    Bowling Green (II)   Maria Lourdes Gonzales
    Cleveland   Benjamin Tupaz
    Columbus   Aida Jordan
    Toledo   Dr. Antonio Yap

Oregon

    Beaverton   Jaime Lim

Texas

    Dallas   Perry Garcia
    Duncanville   Aristotle Sunio

Virginia

    Norfolk   Resty Serrano

Washington

    Seattle   Edgar Hernandez

Washington, D.C.

                              Dr. Eddie Padlan

Report on a Successful Demonstration

It took a considerable amount of daring to mount a public demonstration against Marcos in the United States. During the early years of resistance organizing, the U.S. administrations approved of his martial law regime, and the majority of Filipino immigrants could not have cared less about it. Thus, when an occasion presented itself as a worthwhile event to show off the bad side of martial law, the MFP pounced on it. Witness how one chapter pulled one off.

Report on a Successful Demonstration

(Minnesota MFP Chapter)

Event: Dedication Ceremony of a Goodwill Airplane for the Philippines North Central Airlines Hangar, MPLS Airport, October 26, 1974.

Our Purpose: To distribute MFP leaflets to Filipino and American guests and picket the appearance of Philippine Ambassador to the U.S. Eduardo Romualdez (brother-in-law of Mrs. Imelda Marcos).

Planning: In anticipation that we would not get into the premises, we prepared a dozen large protest signs, with messages such as "MFP," "Restore Philippine Democracy," "Greetings from the Outlaws to the In-Laws," "Marcos Murderer of Democracy," and "Retire Marcos, Not Freedom."

Literature for mass distribution included "Life under Martial Law," an editorial by Richard Deats, and locally produced leaflets appealing for letters. The local Cultural Society of Filipino Americans (CSFA) was scheduled to sing and dance at the ceremony, which suited our purposes well in that several members were MFP supporters or sympathizers. We discussed "pulling hard capers"—having a

CSFA performer take over a microphone and vehemently protest martial law, or a possible walkout by half of the performers in protest against the dictatorship. But we settled on "soft capers"—the performers would sing "Bayan Ko" while the picketers joined in. One performer would make a short statement. One performer wore an armband of protest. This way we would not alienate the audience, a potential source of sympathetic Americans. And we could woo CSFA members and other Filipinos who were present but not yet with us in spirit.

At the end of the ceremony, when the performers had established themselves in the hearts of the audience, some of them could join the picket lines and help us distribute the literature. We alerted local TV and newspapers that the ceremony would be newsworthy.

What Happened: All of our MFP people were able to stroll right into the airplane hangar itself! We did not display the posters, but a dozen of us were able to pass out the literature to practically every person who entered. About fifteen minutes before the start of the ceremony, the manager caught on, approached us, and told us to leave. We could not hand out the literature; we could not protest on their privately leased property; we had not cleared things with him first; he would call the police if we did not stop.

We handled him superbly. We told him that we were merely passing out educational literature, most of it from the clergy. We said that we were doing this here because it could not be done in the Philippines. We assured him that we were only expressing dissatisfaction with the Marcos government.

Meanwhile, half of us continued to pass out the literature. We talked with him for fifteen minutes, and when he threatened to have the police evict us, I quietly but firmly said that we would leave, but we would throw up a loud, agitated picket line outside the gate. He was over a barrel, because kicking us out would have caused a bigger ruckus than letting us stay. Finally, when all the guests had arrived, I agreed with him that we would hand out no more literature, that we would sit down quietly and not disturb the ceremony. He was quite relieved.

One CSFA member introduced the performers and gave Romualdez a "message to take to Marcos: that Filipinos in Minnesota are anxiously awaiting a quick end to martial law and a restoration of complete civil liberties at home." The entire audience and we protesters responded with hearty applause.

We had planned to hold up our posters in the back of the room during the singing of "Bayan Ko." There were two news teams eager to take our pictures. When the manager saw us readying the posters, he stormed over and objected that we had said we would use no posters. One news team already had a microphone under his chin, and when they started to film, he gave up and left us. When the ceremony ended, we spaced ourselves outside so that people could read each poster on their way out. Smiles and "good days" were well received, although some people were afraid of us.

TV Coverage: One station explained our purpose well and gave us as much time as the ambassador. The other station showed a good deal of our activities, the posters, the cover of "Life under Martial Law," and the interview. However, the interview was very poorly edited, and the only thing they really told people was that we feared that Marcos would use the aircraft for counterinsurgency. This was good for raising suspicions about Marcos, but it was at the expense of the church group.

Points to Remember: (1) Our gentle manner was completely acceptable to all Filipinos present. Most Americans took the literature. Some were very happy to see us, but a few thought that it was "un-Christian" of us to usurp the event.

(2) We remained civil and courteous to the very disturbed manager. Our bullshitting bought precious time, and we gave in a little now and then so that he would feel that he still had control. Some American members of CSFA (looking like slightly paunchy middle-aged businessmen) were of great help when they unexpectedly assisted us in arguing for the right of freedom of expression. He was not quite sure whether he was taking on half the arriving guests or performers. And we did indicate that if some cops were brought in, there would be a far noisier demonstration and picket lines. The TV newsmen really shook him up and tied his hands.

(3) One newsman wanted us to pose nicely with the posters during the ceremony for his convenience in filming. We demurred because we wanted to time it with the song. The song got cut for reasons of time, and we lost a chance for better pictures at that newscast. Play for the newsmen! The other news team gave us great TV time but badly distorted our major intentions. Beware of edited interviews! They may read in more than you want. Make sure they know in twenty words or less why you are there and hand them a one-page press release, so that they will not be confused. Get them to at least say that the Movement for a Free Philippines was there.

Peace—Gary King.

Chronology of Events

The U.S.-based groups opposing martial law initiated local activities to coincide with developments in the Philippines. By doing so, their homeland allies were confident that their resistance campaigns there were being strengthened on the U.S. front, especially with the congressional lobbying.

The Philippine events in this chronology are among those that the U.S.-based groups chose to exploit in their lobbying and outreach activities to Philippine communities, as has been described in more detail in this book.

Dates listed in *italics* refer to the annual and regional conventions of the Movement for a Free Philippines (MFP), during which they mapped out activities related to the events listed during that period. Moreover, for the members, these conventions were vital for keeping morale high, recruiting members, and raising funds. Hence the unbroken regularity of its meetings was a measure of its commitment.

1971	June 21	Constitutional Convention begins work to draft a new charter to replace the 1935 constitution, written during the American colonial period.
1972	July 7	Convention approves a new constitution. It changes the form of government from presidential rule to a parliamentary system and allows President Ferdinand Marcos, whose last and second term was to end in December 1973, to seek a third term.
	September 21	Marcos declares martial law, jails political opponents, closes the legislature, and suspends the constitution.

1973	January 10–15	Plebiscite composed of "citizen assemblies" ratifies new constitution.
	January 17	Marcos signs two decrees extending martial law.
	July 23	National referendum approves Marcos remaining in office beyond December 31.
	July 27	Senator Benigno "Ninoy" Aquino, the most prominent Marcos critic, goes on trial.
	September 22	*MFP first annual convention and founding, Washington, D.C.*
1974	August 9	Gerald Ford assumes the U.S. presidency and serves until January 1977.
	September 22	*MFP annual convention, Chicago, Illinois.*
1975	February 27	Referendum votes to give Marcos continued powers to issue decrees with the force of law. As a result of the vote, the election of an interim National Assembly, as provided by the new constitution, is delayed. Imelda Marcos, the president's wife, is named governor of Metro Manila.
	September 10	*MFP annual convention, Los Angeles, California.*
1976	*September*	*MFP annual convention, St. Louis, Missouri.*
	October 16–17	Referendum approves creation of a National Assembly in place of an interim assembly; amends constitution to allow Marcos to continue exercising martial law powers.
1977	January 20	Jimmy Carter assumes the U.S. presidency and serves until January 1981.
	September	*MFP annual convention, Chicago, Illinois.*
1978	April 6	National elections are held for representatives to the interim National Assembly. Marcos's New Society Party wins 187 seats, as against 13 for the opposition. Aquino, campaigning from his jail cell, loses his bid for a Manila seat to New Society candidate Imelda Marcos. Spontaneous street demonstration by Manila residents, who bang on pots and pans and honk car horns to signify their protest of the fraudulent conduct of the election.
	June 12	Interim National Assembly convenes. Marcos appoints Imelda to new cabinet post as minister of human settlements.
	August	Members of a group calling itself the Light-A-Fire Movement, led by Manila-based businesspeople, bomb Marcos-linked buildings.

1979	September	*MFP annual convention, San Francisco, California.*
1980	January 30	Elections are held for governors and mayors, the first since martial law was imposed. The LABAN and Liberal opposition parties boycott. The New Society party wins 69 of 73 gubernatorial positions and 1,420 of 1,560 mayoral seats.
	April 23	Marcos addresses the 94th Annual Convention of the American Newspaper Association in Honolulu, Hawaii. First visit to the U.S. as president in fourteen years.
	May 8	Aquino is released from prison for medical treatment in the U.S. He was held for seven years and seven months.
	August 22	Nine bombs rock Manila buildings. A group called the April 6 Liberation Movement (in reference to the April 6 street noise demonstration) claims responsibility and warns of more bombings of businesses linked to Marcos. They will set off more bombs on September 12 and October 4. On October 19, a bomb will explode only fifty feet away from Marcos during a convention of the American Society of Travel Agents.
	August 29	*MFP annual convention, Detroit, Michigan.*
1981	January 17	Marcos officially ends nine years of martial law but retains power to impose decrees such as detention of people suspected of subversion and rebellion.
	January 20	Ronald Regan assumes the U.S. presidency and serves until January 1989.
	June 16	Marcos is reelected president for a six-year term. At his June 30 inauguration, Vice President George Bush praises him for "adherence to democracy."
	September	*MFP annual convention, New York City.*
1982	*February*	*MFP regional council, Washington, D.C.*
	June	*MFP regional council, San Francisco, California.*
	September	*MFP regional council, Washington, D.C.*
	September 16	Marcos begins fifteen-day state visit to the U.S.
1983	*May*	*MFP regional council, New York City.*
	August 21	Aquino returns to Manila and is assassinated upon arrival at the airport.
	September	*MFP regional council, Chicago, Illinois.*
	December 18	*Washington Post* report casts doubt on war medals awarded to Marcos.

1984	*January*	*MFP regional council, San Francisco, California.*
	May 14	Elections are held for the National Assembly. Opposition parties win 56 seats out of 183, gaining substantial number over 1978 elections.
	May 19–20	*MFP regional council, Washington, D.C.*
	October 6	*MFP regional council, St. Louis, Missouri.*
1985	*March 2–3*	*MFP regional council, Los Angeles, California.*
	July	*MFP regional council, Toronto, Canada.*
	October	*MFP regional council, Washington, D.C.*
	November 3	Marcos suddenly announces "snap" presidential elections.
	December 3	Aquino's widow, Corazon, declares candidacy for the elections.
1986	*January*	*MFP regional council, San Diego, California.*
	January 23	*New York Times* report questions Marcos's wartime record.
	February 7	Marcos claims victory in snap elections, but vote count favors Aquino in voting marred by massive fraud.
	February 19	Military leaders mutiny against Marcos; Manila residents rally with them and mass toward Presidential Palace.
	February 24	Reagan offers asylum to Marcos.
	February 26	Corazon Aquino takes oath as president. Marcos, his wife and children, and close associates are flown by U.S. helicopter to Guam.

Index

A native of the Philippines, **JOSE V. FUENTECILLA** emigrated to the United States in the 1960s. He has lived and worked as a journalist and editor in New York City.

THE ASIAN AMERICAN EXPERIENCE

The University of Illinois Press
is a founding member of the
Association of American University Presses.

———————————————————————

Composed in 10.5/13 Adobe Minion Pro
with Trade Gothic display
by Jim Proefrock
at the University of Illinois Press
Manufactured by Sheridan Books, Inc.

University of Illinois Press
1325 South Oak Street
Champaign, IL 61820-6903
www.press.uillinois.edu